THE LITTLE BOOK OF
BOND

Written by Michael Heatley and Mike Gent

THE LITTLE BOOK OF
BOND

This edition first published in the UK in 2008
By Green Umbrella Publishing

© Green Umbrella Publishing 2008

www.gupublishing.co.uk

Publishers Jules Gammond and Vanessa Gardner

Printed and bound in Italy

ISBN 978-1906229-87-0

Contents

Chapter 1

The History of Bond

From creation to Quantum…the whole story

THE CREATOR OF JAMES BOND, Ian Fleming, was born in Mayfair, London on 28 May 1908, the second of four sons. His father Valentine, a Conservative MP, was killed in the First World War, shortly before Ian's ninth birthday, leaving his formidable widow Eve (nicknamed "M" by her sons) in charge of the family. A rebellious, moody but charming boy, Ian attended Eton where he was a distinguished athlete but lived in the shadow of his brilliant elder brother Peter. In 1926, at his mother's insistence, he enrolled for officer training at the Royal Military College at Sandhurst. Finding the strict regime absurd, he left in September 1927 without taking a commission.

Fleming was sent to a private finishing school in Kitzbühel in the Austrian Tyrol, where he wrote his first short story, then attended the Universities of Munich and Geneva, studying German and French. Returning to England, he failed the Foreign Office's entrance exam for the diplomatic service before taking a job at the international news agency Reuters when he was 23. In 1933, he was sent to Moscow to cover the trial of six British subjects charged with spying. Later that year, he resigned from Reuters to become a stockbroker.

On the outbreak of the Second World War in 1939, Fleming was headhunted for a job in Naval Intelligence, as personal assistant to the director. He quickly attained the status of commander – the same rank as James Bond.

As with his Russian sojourn, Fleming's wartime experiences provided him with a great deal of material for his novels.

After being discharged, Fleming became foreign manager at Kemsley Newspapers, publisher of the *Sunday Times*, which allowed him to travel abroad frequently on assignments. In 1953 he took charge of Atticus, the paper's equivalent of a gossip column. Fleming had visited Jamaica for a conference in 1944 and was so enchanted by

the island that he bought some land overlooking the ocean and built a house, Goldeneye, there. Fleming accepted the job at Kemsley's on condition that he be allowed two months paid holiday per year, allowing him to escape the English winter by spending every January and February in Jamaica. From 1952 until his death in 1964, he would use the vacation to write a Bond book.

Fleming joked that the first novel, *Casino Royale*, was written as a reaction to marrying for the first time at 43. His wife, Anne, was one of many women in his life. Their affair began during the war and continued after she married Viscount Rothermere in 1945. When Anne became pregnant with the couple's only child, Caspar in 1952, she divorced Rothermere.

Fleming had been harbouring the notion of writing "the spy story to end all spy stories" for several years. Antecedents included Rudyard Kipling's 1901 novel *Kim* and works by Dornford Yates, William Le Queux and E Phillips Oppenheim. Fleming was also influenced by John Buchan, author of *The*

Thirty-nine Steps, W Somerset Maugham's *Ashenden* series and HC "Sapper" McNeile's patriotic hero *Bulldog Drummond*.

Although many role models for Bond have been suggested, including Peter Fleming who himself published a novel in 1951 and helped secure *Casino Royale* a berth at publishers Cape, the character most likely represented an idealised version of Ian Fleming himself. 007 and his creator shared many of the same tastes in cigarettes, clothes, food and women, whilst Bond's appearance was based on American composer/musician Hoagy Carmichael.

Casino Royale, published in April 1953, was a notable success for a first novel and was followed by 13 more books, including two volumes of short stories. The Bond books were generally well-received by the critics – who dubbed the author's vigorous style the "Fleming Sweep" – and popular with the public, but the literary establishment sneered at them. Fleming had an ambivalent relationship with his creation, referring to Bond as "a blunt instrument" and "a cardboard booby". He dallied with killing 007 off at the end of *From Russia With Love* but, of course,

the secret agent returned.

Aware of the screen potential of his creation, Fleming made several attempts to bring Bond to the cinema or television. The first adaptation was *Casino Royale* which appeared on US

television in 1954, starring Barry Nelson as an American "Jimmy" Bond. The following year, Fleming sold the film rights for *Casino Royale* to producer Charles K Feldman, resulting in a spoof Bond film in 1967. A deal for the rest of the novels was finally made in 1961 with Eon Productions, the production partnership of Cubby Broccoli and Harry Saltzman.

The series began with *Dr No* in 1962, with the relatively unknown Sean Connery in the lead role. The box-office success of the movies reignited interest in Fleming's novels and spawned a host of imitators. Having survived a heart attack in 1961, Fleming declined to compromise his lifestyle which included considerable amounts of cigarettes and alcohol. He suffered a second, fatal coronary in August 1964, before he could revise the first draft of *The Man With the Golden Gun.*

Shortly after his death, the third 007 film, *Goldfinger,* was released, setting Bond-mania in motion. James Bond became one of the world's best-known fictional characters and the movies became the most successful and longest-running series in movie history, periodically renewing and reinventing itself as George Lazenby, Roger Moore, Timothy Dalton, Pierce Brosnan and Daniel Craig succeeded Connery over the years.

Fleming had transferred his copyright in Bond to Glidrose Productions which authorised new 007 novels after his death and English novelist and Bond buff Kingsley Amis, writing as Robert Markham, produced *Colonel Sun* in 1968. Apart from novelisations *The Spy Who Loved Me* and *Moonraker* (as the films were radically different from the novels), 13 years elapsed before the next new Bond book when British thriller writer John Gardner stepped into Fleming's shoes in 1981. He was replaced in 1997 by American Bond expert and screenwriter Raymond Benson.

When Benson resigned in 2002, the company (now known as Ian Fleming Publications and run by the author's family) chose comic actor Charlie Higson to create a series of five prequels featuring "Young Bond". To mark the centenary of Fleming's birth, the adult Bond returned to action in 2008. *Devil May Care* by British novelist Sebastian Faulks is set in 1967 after the events of *The Man With The Golden Gun*, Fleming's final novel.

RIGHT A selection of James Bond books

Book List

By Ian Fleming

- *Casino Royale* (1953)
- *Live And Let Die* (1954)
- *Moonraker* (1955)
- *Diamonds Are Forever* (1956)
- *From Russia With Love* (1957)
- *Doctor No* (1958)
- *Goldfinger* (1959)
- *For Your Eyes Only* (Short Stories) (1960)
- *Thunderball* (1961)
- *The Spy Who Loved Me* (1962)
- *On Her Majesty's Secret Service* (1963)
- *You Only Live Twice* (1964)
- *The Man With The Golden Gun* (1965)
- *Octopussy And The Living Daylights* (Short Stories) (1966)

By Robert Markham (Kingsley Amis)

- *Colonel Sun* (1968)

By Christopher Wood

- *James Bond, The Spy Who*
- *Loved Me* (1977)
- *James Bond And Moonraker* (1979)

By John Gardner

- *Licence Renewed* (1981)
- *For Special Services* (1982)
- *Icebreaker* (1983)
- *Role Of Honour* (1984)
- *Nobody Lives Forever* (1986)
- *No Deals Mr Bond* (1987)
- *Scorpius* (1988)
- *Win Lose Or Die* (1989)
- *Licence To Kill* (Novelisation) (1989)
- *Brokenclaw* (1990)
- *The Man From Barbarossa* (1991)
- *Death Is Forever* (1992)
- *Never Send Flowers* (1993)
- *Seafire* (1994)
- *Goldeneye* (Novelisation) (1995)
- *Cold* (*Coldfall* In The Us) (1996)

By Raymond Benson

- *Zero Minus Ten* (1997)
- *Tomorrow Never Dies* (Novelisation)(1997)
- *The Facts Of Death* (1998)
- *High Time To Kill* (1999)
- *The World Is Not Enough* (Novelisation) (1999)
- *Doubleshot* (2000)
- *Never Dream Of Dying* (2001)
- *Die Another Day* (Novelisation) (2002)
- *The Man With The Red Tattoo* (2002)

By Charlie Higson

- *Silverfin* (2005)
- *Blood Fever* (2006)
- *Double Or Die* (2007)
- *Hurricane Gold* (2007)
- *By Royal Command* (2008)

By Sebastian Faulks

- *Devil May Care* (2008)

Chapter 2

The Actors

CASTING THE HERO WAS CRUCIAL for the success of the James Bond series. Various actors were in the frame: Ian Fleming favoured David Niven – who, like Cary Grant, was too big for the modest budget – whilst Roger Moore, Richard Burton and Patrick McGoohan were in contention. The *Daily Express* newspaper, then serialising Fleming's novels in comic-strip form, conducted a poll for its readers' choice as 007, which Sean Connery topped. The rest, including his five successors, is movie history!

Sean Connery	
Date of Birth:	25 August 1930
Place of Birth	Edinburgh, Scotland
Height	6' 1½"
Colour of eyes	Brown
Weight	*Dr No* (1961) 177lbs *Never Say Never Again* (1983) 190lbs
Date of first Bond	1962
Number of Bond films	Seven
Retired	1967, 1971 and 1983

Sean Connery

THE FIRST AND, FOR MANY, THE definitive screen Bond, Sean Connery was born Thomas Sean Connery. He started work, aged nine, delivering milk and left school at 13 after which

ABOVE Sean Connery, the first big-screen James Bond in *From Russia With Love*

he was employed as a milkman, labourer, cement mixer and coffin polisher. At 16, he joined the Royal Navy, further honing his athletic physique by boxing and weightlifting. Discharged after three years because of a duodenal ulcer, he became a male model at Edinburgh School of Art.

Co-producer Cubby Broccoli was won over after seeing him in the Disney film *Darby O'Gill And The Little People*, particularly impressed by his light-footed grace – unusual in such a tall man – and range of acting experience. Crucially, Broccoli's wife highlighted Connery's appeal to women. Fleming was initially dismayed at the choice but changed his mind after seeing the movie.

Dr No director Terence Young had worked previously with Connery and initially shared some of Fleming's misgivings that the actor had too many rough edges for the part. Under Young's tutelage Connery learnt to apply a veneer of sophistication over his harsh Scottish exterior. Young and Connery were also largely responsible for injecting humour into 007.

By *You Only Live Twice*, Connery was weary of the role; his frustrations

LEFT Sean Connery with Eunice Gayson as Sylvia Trench in *Dr No*

RIGHT Sean Connery rehearses a bedroom scene with actress Daniela Bianchi in *From Russia With Love*

were exacerbated by long production schedules and frequent delays. The final straw was the constant invasion of his privacy during the making of *You Only Live Twice*.

After the box-office disappointments of *On Her Majesty's Secret Service* with George Lazenby in the title role, United Artists tempted Connery to return by offering him over £1 million – a huge sum for 1971 which he used to set up the Scottish International Educational Trust charity. The actor's seventh and final screen outing as the secret agent came in the unofficial 1983 Bond movie *Never Say Never Again*.

Disillusionment with the studio system caused Connery to take a break from acting for three years. Roles in *The Name Of The Rose* and *Highlander* reignited his career. He went on to win an Oscar for best supporting actor in 1987 for his role as an Irish cop in *The Untouchables*. Connery also made memorable appearances in *The Hunt For Red October*, *The Russia House*, *The Rock* and *Entrapment*, maintaining his distinctive Scottish burr whatever the nationality of his character.

Twice married, to actress Diane

RIGHT George
Lazenby, the second
James Bond

George Lazenby

Cilento in 1962, mother of his actor son Jason, and later to French artist Micheline Roquebrune, Connery has lived abroad for many years. Despite his criticisms of the British establishment, he accepted a knighthood in July 2000.

His association with Bond was revived in 2005 when he recorded the character's voice and permitted his likeness (1963 version) to be used for 007 in the video game version of From Russia With Love.

George Lazenby	
Date of Birth:	5th September 1939
Place of Birth	New South Wales, Australia
Height	6' 2"
Colour of eyes	Brown
Weight	186lbs
Date of first Bond	1969
Number of Bond films	One
Retired	1969

THE "FORGOTTEN" BOND, GEORGE Lazenby worked as a car salesman and ski instructor before joining the Australian Army Special Forces where he taught unarmed combat. After moving to London in 1964, he became the world's highest-paid male model and gained notoriety in a Fry's chocolate television commercial.

When the part of Bond was being cast in 1968, Lazenby set about accentuating his resemblance to Sean Connery, purchasing a suit from the same tailor and having his hair cut in a similar way. Coincidentally, Cubby Broccoli was in the next chair at the barbers' and remembered him when auditions took place. It took four months of rigorous testing to convince the producers that Lazenby could meet the demands of the role.

Lazenby found it difficult not only stepping into Connery's shoes but also in dealing with the sudden glare of the media spotlight. Rumours of a fall-out with On Her Majesty's Secret Service co-star Diana Rigg were played down but Lazenby admitted that he felt

compelled to act the part of Bond off screen as well as on.

Declining to sign a seven-film contract for Bond, Lazenby gambled on establishing himself as an actor after only one movie and came to regret the decision. His self-financed 1971 movie *Universal Soldier* was rarely seen. Disaster struck in 1973 when Bruce Lee died before Lazenby could appear in a projected series of martial arts films with him. He made a cameo appearance as the Aston Martin-driving "JB" in the 1983 TV movie *The Return Of The Man From UNCLE*.

Lazenby has since made occasional forays into acting but became wealthy through property development. In 2002, he married his second wife, former tennis player Pam Shriver, with whom he has three children.

Roger Moore

DEBUTING IN 1973'S *LIVE AND LET Die*, Roger Moore was the first English actor to play Bond. Moore attended RADA after completing his national service but found acting work hard to come by and found employment as a male model. Despite winning a contract with MGM in America, Moore's early movies were flops and it was on television that he became well-known, starring as the hero of the serial *Ivanhoe* and appearing in *Maverick*. In 1961, he was cast in the title role of ATV's adaptation of Leslie Charteris' *Saint* books, a series that ran until 1967.

His commitment to *The Saint* precluded him from serious consideration as James Bond when the role was first available, although he was on the short-

Roger Moore	
Date of Birth:	14 October 1927
Place of Birth	Stockwell, London
Height	6' 1"
Colour of eyes	Blue
Weight	180lbs
Date of first Bond	1973
Number of Bond films	Seven
Retired	1985

list. His action hero credentials were further advanced by *The Persuaders* television series made by Lew Grade's ATV in 1971 which co-starred Tony Curtis.

The show's failure in America meant that Moore was available for Bond the following year. Although United Artists favoured casting a big-name American star, Eon Productions insisted that 007 had to be British and Moore was the only serious contender.

The star of seven consecutive Bond movies, Moore was the longest-running 007 although his light touch did not always endear him to the critics or to Bond purists. He was the oldest Bond, 45 when cast and 57 when shooting his last 007 movie *A View To A Kill*.

He has been married four times, firstly at 19 to ice skater Doorn Van Steyn, then in 1953 to singer Dorothy Squires, whom he left in 1961 for Italian actress Luisa Mattioli, and finally to Kristina Tholstrup in 1993. Since Bond, Moore has worked tirelessly for the United Nations Children's charity UNICEF and was knighted in June 2003 for his efforts.

LEFT Roger Moore and the Bond Girls from *A View to A Kill*

Timothy Dalton

THE INTENSE, BROODING BOND, Timothy Dalton grew up in Belper, Derbyshire. His interest in acting began at Grammar School and he joined the local amateur dramatic society before enrolling at RADA in 1964. He toured with the National Youth Theatre and worked with the Birmingham Repertory Theatre in 1966. Dalton's television debut was in the 1967 series *Saturday While Sunday.* The following year, he appeared in his first of several movie roles, *The Lion In Winter.*

Dalton was a front-runner to succeed Sean Connery as Bond but withdrew, believing himself too young for the role. Although not approached when Roger Moore was cast in 1972, he was sounded out by Cubby Broccoli about taking over should Moore decline to return in *For Your Eyes Only.* Dalton again demurred, unimpressed at the direction the Bond movies were taking.

In between brushes with 007, Dalton worked with the Royal Shakespeare Company and his film roles included a gay British Embassy official in the spy movie *Permission To Kill.* On British tel-

Timothy Dalton	
Date of Birth:	21 March 1948
Place of Birth	Colwyn Bay, Wales
Height	6' 2"
Colour of eyes	Green
Weight	*The Living Daylights* (1987) 173lbs *Licence To Kill* (1989) 187lbs
Date of first Bond	1987
Number of Bond films	Two
Retired	1994

evision, he acted in adaptations of *Jane Eyre* and *The Master Of Ballantrae.* In America, he was cast as a Bond-like character in *Charlie's Angels,* before finally agreeing to play the genuine article in *The Living Daylights.* At 6' 2", with dark, chiselled features and dimpled chin, Dalton had the right image. He re-read Fleming's books as preparation and consulted them on set to ensure that his Bond was as authentic as possible.

Following *Licence To Kill,* legal battles

LEFT Timothy Dalton

between UA/MGM and Eon rumbled on until Dalton's contract expired. Although negotiations were underway to renew it, Dalton announced an amicable parting of the ways in April 1994. Since then he has acted extensively in the theatre, on television and in movies. He is unmarried and lives in Los Angeles.

Pierce Brosnan

THE FIFTH JAMES BOND, IRISHMAN Pierce Brosnan moved to London in 1964. He studied commercial illustration before switching to acting in 1973, training at the Drama Centre. His theatre debut came in a 1976 production of *Wait Until Dark* at the Theatre Royal, York. The following year, playwright Tennessee Williams chose Brosnan for the part of McCabe in the British premiere of *The Red Devil Battery Sign*. Television beckoned in the shape of *The Professionals* and *Hammer House Of Horror* and his first movie appearance was in 1980's *The Long Good Friday*.

He earned a Golden Globe nomination for best supporting actor in BBC

Pierce Brosnan	
Date of Birth:	16th May 1953
Place of Birth	County Meath, Ireland
Height	6' 1"
Colour of eyes	Blue
Weight	*GoldenEye* (1995) 164lbs *Die Another Day* (2002) 211lbs
Date of first Bond	1995
Number of Bond films	Four
Retired	2004

television's 1982 series *Nancy Astor* and moved to America following his first US television role in *Mansions Of America*, becoming internationally famous as *Remington Steele*. Brosnan first encountered Cubby Broccoli in Corfu on location for *For Your Eyes Only* in which his wife Cassandra Harris, who died of cancer in 1991, was appearing. Broccoli instantly earmarked him as a potential successor to Roger Moore. Although *Remington Steele* had apparently ended

LEFT Pierce Brosnan, the fifth James Bond

in 1986, the makers held him to his contract when Eon's interest in Brosnan became public which meant that he missed out on Bond. In 1994, he was first choice to play his dream role.

Waiting for nine years had worked to his advantage. Indeed, he remarked that "it's a role better suited to someone in his forties". After four hugely successful Bond movies, negotiations for more were underway until Brosnan announced in 2004 that he was quitting. Like Sean Connery, he "returned" to the character when his voice and likeness were used for a Bond-based computer game.

Now married to American journalist Keely Shaye Smith, Brosnan appeared in the 2008 movie adaptation of the Abba musical *Mamma Mia*.

Daniel Craig

STOCKY AND FAIR-HAIRED, DANIEL Craig did not seem to fit the image of James Bond as tall, dark and suave but he silenced detractors with his convincing portrayal of Ian Fleming's "blunt instrument". Brought up on the Wirral, Craig's interest in acting began at school. At 16 he successfully auditioned for the National Youth Theatre and toured with them in Spain and Russia. After several failed attempts he was admitted to the Guildhall School of Music and Drama in 1988. Three years later, he graduated, making his film debut in *The Power Of One* in 1992.

Craig's acting career continued on television with appearances in *Sharpe's Eagle*, *Drop The Dead Donkey* and a starring role in the acclaimed BBC TV drama *Our Friends In The North* (1996). International recognition arrived after leading roles in *Lara Croft: Tomb Raider* (2001) and *Road To Perdition* (2002). Rather than following the superstar route, Craig opted for testing and sometimes quirky roles in *The Mother* (2003), *Layer Cake* (2004) and *Enduring Love* (2004). Unveiled in October 2005 as the new Bond, Craig weathered a storm of protests from purists although four of his predecessors – Connery, Moore, Dalton and Brosnan – lent their support. Location photographs of the shirtless actor also convinced many female Bond fans that he was ideal for the job.

Craig brought an emotional depth to James Bond; in *Casino Royale* he por-

Daniel Craig	
Date of Birth:	2 March 1968
Place of Birth	Chester
Height	5' 11"
Colour of eyes	Blue
Weight	165lbs
Date of first Bond	2006
Number of Bond films	Two
Retired	Not yet!

trayed a raw secret agent, making mistakes whilst learning the ropes and *Quantum Of Solace* continued Bond's learning curve. Despite the media furore surrounding Bond movies, Craig prefers to remain a low-key figure. In 1992 he married Scottish actress Fiona Loudon and became a father. The couple divorced in 1994 and his current partner is Japanese-American film producer Satsuki Mitchell, who accompanied him to the *Casino Royale* premiere.

LEFT Daniel Craig attends the world premiere of the 21st James Bond movie, *Casino Royale*

Chapter 3

Bond Girls

THE IMAGE IS OF A WELL-ENDOWED bimbo, but in fact Bond girls are a more diverse bunch. Not necessarily the incapable little lady who needs rescuing, the common element is that they all fall for Bond…sooner or later. And did we mention they are all stunningly beautiful?

The silly, suggestive names begin with *Goldfinger*'s Pussy Galore, but Ian Fleming did not come up with many of these. He went for the exotic/evocative and it was the screenwriters who came up with the rather more explicit likes of Holly Goodhead (*Moonraker*) and Plenty O'Toole (*Diamonds Are Forever*).

Little-known Swiss actress Ursula Andress remains the definitive Bond girl, her appearance in the white bikini in *Dr No* one of the sexiest moments in cinema. She cast a long shadow on those who followed.

Before Ursula made her unforgettable entrance, the first Bond girl on screen was Eunice Gayson as Sylvia Trench who meets Bond at the baccarat table and feeds him the iconic name line. She was to have appeared in the first six Bonds but in the event only returned in *From Russia With Love*, and became the only Bond girl to play the same role in two films.

The employment of beauty queens like Daniela Bianchi (*From Russia With Love*) and Claudine Auger (*Thunderball*) proved less than fruitful. Their dialogue had to be dubbed, and they enjoyed minimal post-Bond careers - though the fact both married millionaires may have had something to do with this! Likewise the two Japanese actresses from *You Only Live Twice*, Akiko Wakabayashi and Mie Hama, only appeared in Western films once. They swapped roles during production;

Akiko ended up as secret agent Aki, the film's sacrificial lamb, while Mie starred as Kissy Suzuki, Bond's Japanese "bride" who resists his overtures until the mission is completed.

Two British Bond girls to grace the

role were Diana Rigg and Honor Blackman. Both of course had starred in TV's *Avengers*, Rigg as Emma Peel (1965-1968) and Blackman as Cathy Gale (1962-1964).

The Royal Shakespeare Company-trained Rigg, was brought in to provide some thespian weight to *On Her Majesty's Secret Service*, and was the first to really break the Bond girl mould. It was something of a role reversal with the non-actor playing 007 rather than the girl, and she is to date the only woman to become Mrs James Bond. Rigg shook off "the curse" of the Bond girl (the belief that they would be type-cast and subsequently achieve little) and continued her highly respected career.

Blackman, as *Goldfinger*'s Pussy Galore, was a bit more "liberated". She utilised the karate-chopping skills she learned as Cathy Gale in *The Avengers* and performed most of her own stunts, despite being, at 37, the oldest Bond girl. Also in *Goldfinger* was Shirley Eaton (Jill Masterson), who supplied an unforgettable image when her naked body was covered in gold. Another British actress, Caroline Munro, had a small but fondly remembered role in *The Spy Who Loved Me*.

As with the girls that married millionaires, being a Bond girl could have real-life romantic repercussions. *The Spy Who Loved Me* star Barbara Bach's acting career tailed off after she married Ringo Starr, while Britt Ekland began a relationship with rock star Rod Stewart the year after starring in 1974's *The Man With The Golden Gun*. On a different tack, Maud Adams, who also graced *Golden Gun*, was so impressive as the villain's treacherous lover that she was invited back to star in *Octopussy* – the second Bond girl to appear twice.

Bond girls are rarely in line for Oscars, though they have been known to make an appearance on the red carpet. Halle Berry, the former beauty queen who starred in *Die Another Day*, is the exception that proves the rule. She was presented with an Oscar for *Monster's Ball* during the making of her only Bond movie, in which she reprised the Ursula Andress bikini scene to the delight of teenage boys…and their fathers!

Eva Green's appearance as Vesper Lynd in *Casino Royale* ended in her becoming the second main Bond girl to be bumped off. This allowed the follow-up, *Quantum Of Solace* to revive the revenge motif of the novel *You Only Live Twice* but ensured her tenure as a Bond girl would be strictly a one-off.

Bond films just wouldn't be Bond films without the female of the species – here's to many more.

LEFT Ursula Andress, the quintessential Bond girl in her striking bikini

BELOW Diana Rigg played the part of Tracy di Vicenzo, the only true love of Bond's life

Chapter 4

The Movies

RIGHT 1962, The first James Bond movie: *Dr No*

THE ODDS OF BOND BECOMING A worldwide phenomenon looked long indeed when the movie series was first mooted in the early Sixties. Indeed, its producers struggled to obtain finance for a Bond film from the major American studios whose executives feared the books were too British and too sexual for Stateside audiences. Nearly half a century later, we remain shaken and stirred by the ultimate all-action big-screen espionage phenomenon.

Dr No (1962-63)

DIRECTED BY TERENCE YOUNG, *Dr No* introduced many soon to be familiar elements of Bond's world including the recurring characters of M (Bernard Lee), Miss Moneypenny (Lois Maxwell) and Bond's occasional American ally Felix Leiter, played by Jack Lord. The movie is mostly faithful to the novel, but one vital difference is the replacement of the Russian counter-intelligence organisation SMERSH with the international terrorist group SPECTRE.

007 is sent to Jamaica to investigate the

Dr No	
Bond Film Number	One
Year released	1962 UK
Starring	Sean Connery
Director	Terence Young
Score	Monty Norman
Filmed In	Jamaica, Pinewood Studios
Budget	$1,000,000
Box Office Gross	$59,600,000

disappearance of a British agent. The trail leads him to Dr No's headquarters, the island of Crab Key. Here, Bond encounters Honey Ryder, played by Ursula Andress, who sparked the whole Bond girl phenomenon by simply walking out of the sea in a white bikini. The pair are captured by the maniacal Dr No (Joseph Wiseman) who is plotting to destroy the American space programme. Bond overcomes a series of death traps before turning his antagonist's scheme against him, destroying his base and escaping with Honey.

Dr No was, in many respects, grittier and more realistic than its immediate successors. The violence was less stylised, including the famously controversial scene where Bond shoots Professor Dent in cold blood. Gadgetry, such a mainstay of Bond movies to come, was absent as our man has to rely on his wits to survive and the cinematic 007 displayed a better-developed sense of humour than his literary counterpart. Premiering in the UK in October 1962 and in America the following May, *Dr No* earned enough in box-office receipts in

Britain alone to recoup the modest $1 million budget granted by United Artists, ensuring that James Bond would indeed return.

From Russia With Love (1963)

BOND'S POPULARITY IN AMERICA was boosted when President John F Kennedy named *From Russia With Love* as one of his top 10 favourite books, making it an obvious choice for adaptation as the second 007 movie. The film was largely faithful to the novel although overlaying SPECTRE onto the activities of SMERSH seemed an unnecessary complication to a straightforward spy story. Bond was lured into a trap with a decoding machine and, crucially, a beautiful girl as the inducements.

Along with director Terence Young, most of the same production crew who worked on the previous film returned for *From Russia With Love*, although there was no place for Ken Adam's high-tech set designs in this more realistic tale. The budget was higher than for *Dr No*, as the producers aimed for a bigger and better spectacle. Location filming took place in the story's Istanbul setting, but problems with the boat chase required some re-shooting in England.

Sean Connery was maturing into the

From Russia With Love	
Bond Film Number	Two
Year released	1963
Starring	Sean Connery
Director	Terence Young
Score	John Barry
Filmed In	Turkey, Pinewood Studios
Budget	$2,500,00
Box Office Gross	$78,900,000

central role and he was ably supported by a strong cast. Pedro Armendariz excelled as Bond's Turkish ally Kerim Bey, although he was terminally ill when the film was being made. A former Miss Rome, Daniela Bianchi, was a novice at acting but gave an honest performance (although her dialogue was dubbed) as Tatiana Romanova, the bait in the honeytrap. Robert Shaw and Lotte Lenya breathed malevolent life into deadly duo Red Grant and Rosa Klebb. The mastermind of SPECTRE referred to only as "number one" remained a shadowy presence.

Co-screenwriter Richard Maibaum cited *From Russia With Love* as his favourite Bond movie, as did Terence Young and Sean Connery. Its international success confirmed that the cinematic Bond was not merely a British phenomenon but was poised to become a Sixties icon.

FAR LEFT 1963, The second James Bond movie: *From Russia With Love*

LEFT 1964, The third James Bond movie: *Goldfinger*

Goldfinger	
Bond Film Number	Three
Year released	1964
Starring	Sean Connery
Director	Guy Hamilton
Score	John Barry
Filmed In	Switzerland, USA, Pinewood Studios
Budget	$3,500,000
Box Office Gross	$124,900,000

Goldfinger (1964)

RIGHT 1965, The fourth James Bond movie: *Thunderball*

GOLDFINGER WAS THE FIRST BOND blockbuster, its box-office receipts justifying every penny of United Artists' expensive publicity campaign. The 007 phenomenon began here as the movie ignited a merchandising frenzy and sent book sales into overdrive when it premiered, ironically, a month after Ian Fleming's death.

With Terence Young unavailable, Guy Hamilton took the director's chair for the first of his four Bond movies, fashioning a slick, sophisticated thriller with an increased emphasis on humour, starting with a pre-credits sequence which had no relevance to the main story. Ken Adam's return as set designer was distinguished by his imaginative version of Fort Knox.

The shortcomings of the literary *Goldfinger* are improved upon by scriptwriters Richard Maibaum and Paul Dehn. The villain planned to irradiate the American gold reserves rather than steal it which, according to 007 in the movie, would have taken 12 weeks. *Goldfinger* featured three Bond girls, Shirley Eaton (Jill Masterson), Tania Mallet plays her sister Tilly, and Honor Blackman as Pussy Galore.

The pairing of Gert Frobe as Auric Goldfinger and Harold Sakata as his henchman Oddjob was inspired casting. Oddjob will be remembered for his steel-rimmed bowler hat which 007 uses to electrocute him at the climax of their battle in the vault of Fort Knox.

Goldfinger upped the ante in terms of gadgets, gimmicks and cars. After its appearance in the film, the Aston Martin DB5 – "the most famous car in the world" – became a best-selling Corgi toy, while the laser beam with which Goldfinger threatens Bond was the first cinematic use, via an optical effect, of what was a futuristic device in 1964. The film drew almost universal praise from the critics and is often cited as the definitive 007 movie, building on the foundations laid in the first two films to set the template later Bonds would follow.

Thunderball (1965)

BIGGER, MORE EXPENSIVE AND EVEN more successful at the box-office than its predecessors, *Thunderball* had a complex history. Ian Fleming had collaborated with film writers Jack Whittingham and Kevin McClory in an abortive attempt to devise a screen treatment for Bond. Fleming used the story they created as the basis for his 1961 novel *Thunderball*. Whittingham and McClory sued for copyright infringement and the case, which adversely affected Fleming's already failing health, was settled in 1962, leaving McClory with the film rights. To head off a rival production, Harry Saltzman and Cubby Broccoli cut a deal with McClory who was credited as producer of *Thunderball* with them as executive producers.

Sticking closely to the original story,

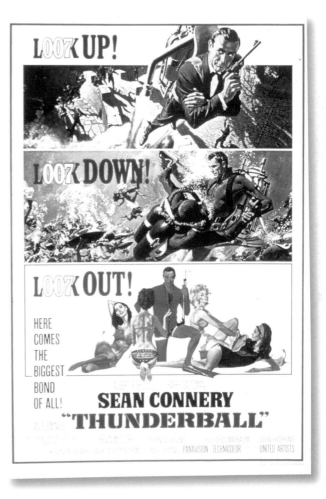

RIGHT 1967, The fifth
James Bond movie: *You
Only Live Twice*

the movie saw Bond travelling to the Bahamas to foil a plot by SPECTRE's second in command, Emilio Largo, to hold the world to ransom by threatening to destroy a major city using stolen nuclear warheads. The movie reached its climax in a lengthy underwater battle scene for which special effects supervisor John Stears won an Oscar for Best Visual Effects. Notwithstanding this accolade, Terence Young, returning for his third and final stint as director, believed that the sub-aqua sequences slowed the pace of the film too much.

Brazilian actor Adolfo Celi played Largo and, as with many foreign actors in Bond movies including main Bond girl Domino, played by former Miss France Claudine Auger, most of his dialogue was dubbed.

The formula established in *Goldfinger* was taken further in *Thunderball*. Although generally well received, some critics complained that the character of James Bond was being swamped by gadgets like the Rocket Belt jet-pack and its underwater equivalent. Nevertheless, *Thunderball* became one of the highest-grossing films of all time, taking £141m at the box-office – a phenomenal sum in 1965 – and the Bond spin-off industry moved into top gear, producing an even more extensive array of merchandising.

Thunderball	
Bond Film Number	Four
Year released	1965
Starring	Sean Connery
Director	Terence Young
Score	John Barry
Filmed In	Paris, Bahamas, Pinewood Studios
Budget	$11,000,000
Box Office Gross	$141,200,000

You Only Live Twice (1967)

RETAINING ONLY THE JAPANESE location and some characters from Ian Fleming's eerie but largely unfilmable novel, *You Only Live Twice* was the most spectacular entry yet into the Bond canon. With Richard Maibaum unavail-

You Only Live Twice	
Bond Film Number	Five
Year released	1967
Starring	Sean Connery
Director	Lewis Gilbert
Score	John Barry
Filmed In	Japan, Pinewood Studios
Budget	$9,500,000
Box Office Gross	$111,600,000

RIGHT 1969, The sixth James Bond movie: *On Her Majesty's Secret Service*

able, the screenplay was by Roald Dahl, a friend of Ian Fleming's but an unusual choice as he was mainly known as a children's writer. Experienced director Lewis Gilbert was at the helm of his first Bond film whilst Sean Connery had made it clear that this was to be his last. The media circus which surrounded much of the overseas filming only served to harden the actor's resolve.

Bond was sent to Japan to discover who was trying to engineer nuclear war by sabotaging the space programmes of both the East and the West. The answer turned out to be SPECTRE, headed by Ernst Stavro Blofeld. Bond saved the day

in an action-packed finale in SPECTRE's hollowed-out volcano, another amazing set design courtesy of Ken Adam.

Three Bond girls had become a pre-requisite by now, with German actress Karin Dor, who played the treacherous Helga Brandt, and Akiko Wakabayashi as Japanese secret agent Aki, meeting early deaths.

Marketing and merchandise remained in overdrive and included toys based on the Toyota 2000 GT car and heavily-armed autogyro "Little Nellie". Mixed notices saw the film praised for its colourful extravagance whilst detractors complained of implausibility and overuse of gadgets. *You Only Live Twice* turned in a healthy profit at the box-office, although the figures were slightly down on *Thunderball*.

This was not enough to concern Eon Productions unduly as the company had bigger problems. Unable to persuade Sean Connery to change his mind about quitting as 007, Cubby Broccoli and Harry Saltzman were forced to seek a replacement for the man, who as the film's publicity posters put it, "IS James Bond".

On Her Majesty's Secret Service (1969)

WITH A NEW ACTOR IN THE TITLE role, the Bond franchise reinvented itself by going back to basics. *On Her Majesty's Secret Service* was a departure from its immediate predecessors, downplaying gadgets and gimmickry in favour of a more human touch. Whereas *You Only Live Twice* had jettisoned most of the source novel, *OHMSS* followed Ian Fleming's story very closely, tragic ending and all.

Having decided that an unknown actor should replace Connery, Broccoli and Saltzman chose 28 year old male model George Lazenby despite his only screen experience being a television commercial. Diana Rigg, famous as Emma Peel in *The Avengers*, was Countess Tracy di Vicenzo, the only woman to become Mrs James Bond whilst Blofeld's unwitting "Angels of Death" included future *New Avengers* star Joanna Lumley.

Whilst searching for his arch-neme-

FAR UP! FAR OUT! FAR MORE! James Bond 007 is back!

ALBERT R. BROCCOLI AND HARRY SALTZMAN

JAMES BOND 007 AN FLEMINGS "ON HER MAJESTY'S SECRET SERVICE"

GEORGE LAZENBY · DIANA RIGG · TELLY SAVALAS
GABRIELE FERZETTI AND ILSE STEPPAT · PANAVISION · TECHNICOLOR · United Artists

On Her Majestys Secret Service	
Bond Film Number	Six
Year released	1969
Starring	George Lazenby
Director	Peter Hunt
Score	John Barry
Filmed In	Switzerland, Pinewood Studios
Budget	$7,000,000
Box Office Gross	$87,4000,000

RIGHT 1971, The seventh James Bond movie: *Diamonds Are Forever*

sis, Bond encounters the rich, troubled Tracy and rescues her from a suicide attempt. Discovering that Blofeld is planning nerve warfare via a group of beautiful girls, from his mountaintop retreat, 007 enlists Tracy's father, head of a crime syndicate, to help foil the plot. The couple were married but, shortly afterwards, Blofeld's hitmen gun down Tracy who dies in Bond's arms.

Graduating from editor and second unit director to take the helm for *OHMSS*, Peter Hunt was responsible for taking Bond back to its roots, fighting to retain the downbeat conclusion. He was ably supported by the return of writer Richard Maibaum whose few changes to the novel, such as upgrading Blofeld's threat from British to global, were improvements.

OHMSS occupies an anomalous position in the Bond canon. Reversing critical opinion at the time of release, many commentators and Bond devotees now regard it as one of the best, if not *the* best Bond movie, but it has been largely overlooked by the general public. Although *OHMSS* was profitable, its failure to match the receipts of the previous two films caused Eon Productions to rethink the direction of the series.

Diamonds Are Forever (1971)

ALTHOUGH AMERICAN ACTOR JOHN Gavin had been signed to succeed George Lazenby, United Artists insisted that Sean Connery be approached, despite his well-publicised aversion to 007. To widespread amazement, Connery accepted. His non-Bond films had not done well and he was in search of funding for his Scottish educational charity, to which he would donate his record-breaking $1.25 million fee. Connery's final official outing as 007 added a wry element of self-parody and was greeted with acclaim.

After the relative failure of *OHMSS*, *Diamonds Are Forever* reintroduced the exaggerated action and humour which made the previous films so successful. The approach again paid off with brisk business at the box-office, particularly in the United States as much of the movie was shot on location in California and Las Vegas. Bond purists, however, felt that the balance had been tipped too far in the direction of humour.

Guy Hamilton returned to the director's chair for the first time since *Goldfinger* and fashioned a string of quickfire set pieces although the finale was criticised as lacklustre. Richard Maibaum's original screenplay was reworked by Tom Manciewicz, resulting in what many feel is the wittiest 007 script.

Bond is sent to investigate disappearing diamonds and follows a smuggling operation (the only vestige of Fleming's original plot). He discovers that his arch-nemesis Blofeld is behind it, planning to use the gems to power a destruc-

Diamonds Are Forever	
Bond Film Number	Seven
Year released	1971
Starring	Sean Connery
Director	Guy Hamilton
Score	John Barry
Filmed In	USA, Germany, Netherlands, France Pinewood Studios
Budget	$7,200,000
Box Office Gross	$116,000,000

RIGHT 1973, The eighth James Bond movie: *Live And Let Die*

tive space laser and hold the world to ransom. 007's other antagonists included the aggressive acrobatic duo Bambi and Thumper (Donna Garrett and Trina Parks) and gay assassins Kidd and Wint (Putter Smith and Bruce Glover). American actress Jill St John was main Bond girl Tiffany Case.

Doubts about the long-term future of the Bond series were assuaged by *Diamonds Are Forever*. The franchise had shown that it was not merely a Sixties phenomenon and that it could be, if not exactly reinvented, then tweaked to keep pace with the times.

Meanwhile, Connery had said "never again", leaving Cubby Broccoli and Harry Saltzman to do battle with United Artists over the casting of the next James Bond.

Live And Let Die (1973)

AN EXTENSIVE PRE-PUBLICITY CAMpaign claiming that Roger Moore was closer to Ian Fleming's original ex-Etonian hero than Sean Connery helped prepare cinema-goers for the new Bond's debut. Eon retained the services of director Guy Hamilton and scriptwriter Tom Manciewicz to create a fast-paced romp which showed that Bond could be adapted for the new decade. In its use of black villains, *Live And Let Die* was influenced by early Seventies blaxploitation movies.

007 is sent to investigate the deaths of three MI6 agents in America where he discovers a plot by Mr Big (Yaphet Kotto), a voodoo-practising gangster, to flood the streets with cheap heroin. Mr Big has dual identity as Dr Kananga, ruler of the Caribbean island of San

Monique. Like *Diamonds Are Forever*, *Live And Let Die* is largely a sequence of spectacular set pieces which included a London bus cut in half when driven under a bridge and a lengthy speedboat chase. The humour is notched up, particularly when redneck sheriff JW Pepper (Clifton James) is on screen. Bond purists complained that, despite the claims about Moore, the film was being aimed at an increasingly younger audience. Again, little of Fleming's novel other than the main characters survived the transition to celluloid.

Jane Seymour was cast in the role of Solitaire after impressing in BBC TV's *The Onedin Line*. Multiple Bond girls was standard practice and there is a brief glimpse of Madeleine Smith as Italian agent Miss Caruso in the scene where M and Moneypenny break with tradition and visit Bond at home. Gloria Hendry plays double agent Rosie Carver, the film's obligatory sacrificial lamb. Yaphet Kotto's menacing Mr Big/Dr Kananga is creepily supported by Julius W Harris as his giggling henchman Tee-Hee, while Geoffrey Holder's Baron Samedi adds a convincing supernatural element to the voodoo scenes.

The box-office performance of *Live*

Live And Let Die	
Bond Film Number	Eight
Year released	1973
Starring	Roger Moore
Director	Guy Hamilton
Score	George Martin
Filmed In	USA, Jamaica, Pinewood Studios
Budget	$7,000,000
Box Office Gross	$161,800,000

And Let Die exceeded *Diamonds Are Forever* and, although the critics were less than convinced about Roger Moore as 007, cinema-goers had no difficulty in accepting him.

The Man With The Golden Gun (1974)

WITH ROGER MOORE SETTLING into the role of Bond and many familiar faces working on it, *The Man With The*

LEFT 1974, The ninth James Bond movie: *The Man With The Golden Gun*

RIGHT 1977, The tenth
James Bond movie: *The
Spy Who Loved Me*

Golden Gun ought to have consolidated the success of *Live And Let Die,* but that did not happen.

Bond is working to recover a device for converting solar energy into electricity when he finds himself the target of infamous assassin Scaramanga (Christopher Lee), the man with the golden gun. This turns out to be a ploy by the villain's mistress Andrea Anders (Maud Adams) to free herself by setting up a duel between 007 and her lover. Scaramanga kills her for sleeping with Bond before 007 duly defeats Scaramanga in his island lair.

Tom Manciewicz wrote the original screenplay, but disagreements with director Guy Hamilton led to long-term Bond scriptwriter Richard Maibaum being brought in to rewrite it. Only the main characters from Fleming's final novel were retained.

Although the film is not regarded as one of the highpoints of the Bond series, Christopher Lee, who turned down the role of *Dr No* in 1962, won praise for his portrayal of the malevolent Scaramanga. 007 does not make an immediate conquest of Bond girl Britt Ekland, the bumbling MI6 agent Mary Goodnight, and their delayed liaison becomes a running joke. Maud Adams was impressive as the villain's treacherous lover, Clifton James' sheriff JW Pepper returns for a comical cameo whilst Roger Moore is his usual suave, unflappable self.

During the making of *The Man With The Golden Gun*, the relationship between co-producers Cubby Broccoli and Harry Saltzman was in the final stages of deterioration and this would be the last movie on which they worked together. The legal and financial fallout threatened the future of both Eon Productions and the Bond franchise. The critics slated *The Man With The Golden*

The Man With the Golden Gun	
Bond Film Number	Nine
Year released	1974
Starring	Roger Moore
Director	Guy Hamilton
Score	John Barry
Filmed In	Hong Kong, Macao, Thailand, Pinewood Studios
Budget	$7,000,000
Box Office Gross	$97,6000,000

Gun and, after a promising start, box-office receipts for the film tailed off. The gross was disappointing for a Bond movie and it seemed as if the traditional pledge that "James Bond will return" might not be fulfilled.

The Spy Who Loved Me (1977)

HIS PARTNERSHIP WITH HARRY Saltzman over, Cubby Broccoli was in sole charge of producing Bond and was determined to take his time to refresh the franchise after the disappointment of *The Man With The Golden Gun*. Ian Fleming had granted the filmmakers the right to use just the title of his 1962 novel *The Spy Who Loved Me*, a controversial work narrated by its heroine with 007 appearing late in the story. There was no option but to devise a completely new story and the script went through a tortuous development process with 14 writers involved.

An added complication was that Blofeld and SPECTRE had to be removed from the draft when Kevin McClory took legal action alleging

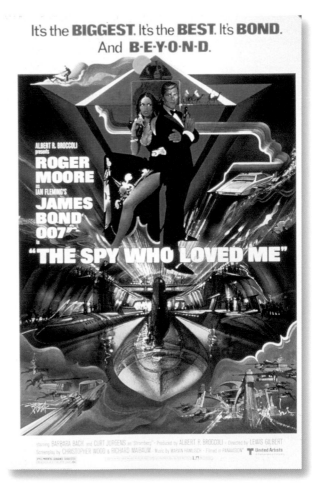

ownership. Backed by United Artists, who doubled the budget, Broccoli sanctioned designer Ken Adam to build the 007 soundstage, the largest in the world, at Pinewood Studios to accommodate the massive set for the movie's climax. These factors combined to delay the making of *The Spy Who Loved Me*.

Eventually credited to Christopher Wood, the screenplay bore strong similarities to *You Only Live Twice*, director Lewis Gilbert's previous Bond film. Stromberg (Kurt Jurgens) is stealing American and Russian nuclear sub-marines with the intention of engineering nuclear war. 007 teams up with a Russian Army major Anya Amasova (Barbara Bach) to foil him. Amasova represented a new, more liberated Bond girl who is virtually 007's equal.

In addition to the plot's resemblance to *You Only Live Twice*, *The Spy Who Loved Me* knowingly referenced other Bonds, containing elements of *Thunderball* (the underwater scenes), *Live And Let Die* and *From Russia With Love* (the fight on the train) and *Goldfinger* (the gadget-laden submersible Lotus Esprit was essentially an update of the Aston Martin DB5).

Broccoli's boldness paid off; *The Spy Who Loved Me* performed admirably against formidable competition in the shape of 1977's summer blockbuster *Star Wars* and was generously reviewed by the majority of critics. Roger Moore cited it as his favourite of the Bond films he starred in.

The Spy Who Loved Me	
Bond Film Number	Ten
Year released	1977
Starring	Roger Moore
Director	Lewis Moore
Score	Marvin Hamlisch
Filmed In	Egypt, Sardinia, Bahamas, Canada, Malta, Scotland, Okinawa, Switzerland, Pinewood Studios
Budget	$14,000,000
Box Office Gross	$185,400,000

Moonraker (1979)

TWICE AS EXPENSIVE AS ITS PRED-ecessor, *Moonraker* was aimed at competing with the post-*Star Wars*

RIGHT 1981, The twelfth James Bond movie: *For Your Eyes Only*

science-fiction boom, although only the film's climax took place in outer space. *For Your Eyes Only* had been announced as the eleventh Bond film but *Moonraker* took its place, the producers utilising Ian Fleming's only remotely sci-fi title. Because of the draconian British tax laws, most of *Moonraker* was made abroad.

Screenwriter Christopher Wood took the name of Fleming's villain and basic notion of the corruption of the space programme to devise the film's plot. Investigating the disappearance of a space shuttle, Bond discovers that millionaire Hugo Drax (Michael Lonsdale) is planning to destroy humanity and replace it with a master race. Teaming up with CIA agent Holly Goodhead (Lois Chiles), Bond thwarts Drax with a little help from a side-swopping Jaws.

Notwithstanding the Pussy Galore homage of her character's name, Lois Chiles continued the trend of the liberated Bond girl established by Barbara Bach. The traditional sacrificial lamb was Drax's personal assistant Corinne Dufour (Corinne Clery) savaged by her employer's Doberman dogs after 007 seduces her into betraying her employer. French actor Michael Lonsdale's Hugo Drax was a sly, scheming villain who enjoyed many of the movie's best lines.

The return of Richard Kiel as Jaws saw the character used as much for slapstick as menace. On a sadder note, the movie saw Bernard Lee's last appearance as M; the actor died in January 1981.

Moonraker was a box-office smash, the highest-grossing Bond movie until overtaken by *GoldenEye* in 1995. It also received good reviews which praised it as a spectacular romp. Die-hard Bond fanatics were less impressed particularly with the climactic scenes, complaining that 007 did not belong in outer space

Moonraker	
Bond Film Number	Eleven
Year released	1979
Starring	Roger Moore
Director	Lewis Gilbert
Score	John Barry
Filmed In	Italy, Brazil, Guatemala, USA, France, Pinewood Studios
Budget	$34,000,000
Box Office Gross	$210,300,000

and that the science-fiction elements were too derivative of the likes of *Star Wars*. Concerns were also expressed that the Bond series was no longer taking itself seriously enough to be entirely credible. Taking these on board, Cubby Broccoli announced that the next film would be returning to basics once more.

For Your Eyes Only (1981)

HAVING TAKEN 007 AS FAR AS POSsible into the fantastic on *Moonraker*, Cubby Broccoli made good on his promise to return the secret agent to something resembling reality with *For Your Eyes Only*. Based on two Fleming short stories, the title piece and *Risico*, the script by long-time Bond writer Richard Maibaum and Michael G Wilson emphasised character and plot whilst remaining relatively gadget-free. The film almost had a new Bond but Roger Moore finally signed just before production began, enticed by a reported seven-figure fee.

Bond is assigned to recover a communications device, the ATAC, which

transmits orders to Polaris nuclear submarines. The Russians are also on its trail. 007 joins forces with Melina Havelock (Carole Bouquet) who is seeking revenge on the killer of her parents, two MI6 agents who were also looking for the device. They find the ATAC but are captured by Kristatos (Julian Glover) who plans to sell it to the Soviets. With the aid of the villain's rival Columbo (Topol), they infiltrate Kristatos' headquarters. 007 ultimately destroys the device rather than let it fall into enemy hands.

Veteran Bond editor/second unit director John Glen stepped up to take the helm, fashioning an exciting action movie and persuading a somewhat reluctant Roger Moore into portraying Bond as a tougher more serious character. The broad humour of previous films is downplayed. The part of the late Bernard Lee as M was rewritten for James Villiers as Tanner, chief of staff. Bond's encounters with women are subtly different – he turns down the advances of teenage Bibi Dahl (Lynn-Holly Johnson) as she is too young and only becomes involved with Melina Havelock at the very end. In between was a liaison with Countess Lisl (played by the late Cassandra Harris, Pierce Brosnan's first wife).

Slightly down on *Moonraker*'s record-breaking receipts, *For Your Eyes Only* topped the British box-office chart for 1981, beating *Raiders Of The Lost Ark.* Critical reaction was generally positive. Eon Productions had been vindicated in the decision to return Bond to its roots.

Octopussy (1983)

ROGER MOORE'S SIXTH OUTING AS Bond faced competition from the unofficial 007 film *Never Say Never Again*. Having tried in vain to stymie the opposition by legal means, Cubby Broccoli devoted his considerable energies to making *Octopussy* a success. The thirteenth Bond film retained the services of director John Glen and the screenplay by Maibaum and Wilson together with *Flashman* author George MacDonald Fraser was loosely based on two posthumously published Ian Fleming short stories.

The rogue Soviet General Orlov (Stephen Berkoff) plans to rekindle the Cold War by setting off a nuclear bomb in West Germany at an American military base thus forcing the US troops to withdraw leaving Europe vulnerable to Russian attack. As cover, Orlov is smuggling Fabergé eggs from the Kremlin in cahoots with wealthy Afghan prince Kamal Khan (Louis Jordan). Khan's business partner, the beautiful Octopussy (Maud Adams), owner of a travelling circus, teams up with Bond to thwart the scheme. Dressed as a clown, 007 defuses the bomb seconds before it is due to explode.

Moore again plays Bond with the tougher characterisation of *For Your*

For Your Eyes Only	
Bond Film Number	Twelve
Year released	1981
Starring	Roger Moore
Director	John Glen
Score	Bill Conti
Filmed In	Greece, Italy, Bahamas, England, Pinewood Studios
Budget	$28,000,000
Box Office Gross	$195,300,000

LEFT 1983, The thirteenth James Bond movie: *Octopussy*

Octopussy	
Bond Film Number	Thirteen
Year released	1983
Starring	Roger Moore
Director	John Glen
Score	John Barry
Filmed In	India, Germany, USA, England, Pinewood Studios
Budget	$27,500,000
Box Office Gross	$187,000,000

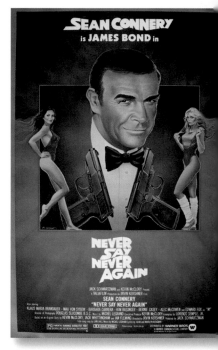

RIGHT 1983, The unoffical James Bond movie: *Never Say Never Again*

Eyes Only. Despite concerns that he was growing too old to convincingly portray 007, the producers were keen to secure the services of their established star in the face of the threat posed by the return of Sean Connery in the rival production. Robert Brown is slightly less crusty than Bernard Lee as the new M whilst Miss Moneypenny has a new young assistant, Penelope Smallbone (Michaela Clavell), a possible replacement who was never seen again.

Octopussy divided opinion. Receiving a battering from the critics on release, it is now regarded as one of the best of the Moore Bonds. Overall, international receipts were slightly down from *For Your Eyes Only* but *Octopussy* grossed more than *Moonraker* in the United States, thanks to its summer release. The two Bond movies did not go into direct competition at the box-office during the summer of 1983, as once looked likely, because of delays to the production of *Never Say Never Again*.

Never Say Never Again (1983)

THE SECOND BOND MOVIE OF 1983 had a complex history and troubled production. As part of his settlement with Ian Fleming, Kevin McClory retained copyright to the material they had co-written. His agreement with Broccoli and Saltzman was not to use any of it for 10 years after *Thunderball* expired in 1976 but legal complications prevented him from raising the necessary finance until former Hollywood lawyer Jack Schwartzman overcame these and secured the rights whilst obtaining backing from Warner Brothers. Even better was persuading the recalcitrant Connery to play 007 once more. The movie's title, an ironic nod to his comments after *Diamonds Are Forever*, was the first use of a non-Fleming title for a Bond film.

Connery was involved at all levels, having approval over script, casting and choice of director. For the latter,

LEFT Sean Connery in typical pose

Never Say Never Again	
Bond Film Number	Unofficial
Year released	1983
Starring	Sean Connery
Director	Irvin Kershner
Score	Michel Legrand
Filmed In	France, Florida, Bahamas, Malta, Monaco, Elstree Studios
Budget	$36,000,000
Box Office Gross	$160,000,000

A View To A Kill	
Bond Film Number	Fourteen
Year released	1985
Starring	Roger Moore
Director	John Glen
Score	John Barry
Filmed In	France, USA, Iceland, Switzerland, Pinewood Studios
Budget	$30,000,000
Box Office Gross	$152,400,000

RIGHT 1985, The official fourteenth James Bond movie: A View To A Kill

governments of the world by threatening to detonate stolen nuclear weapons.

Connery's world-weary 007 is supported by Kim Basinger as Domino and Barbara Carrera as Fatima Blush. Klaus Maria Brandauer is Largo whilst Blofeld is portrayed by Max Von Sydow. Rowan Atkinson makes a cameo appearance as bumbling British agent Nigel Small-Fawcett.

The movie went over budget and, because some re-shooting was necessary, the production dragged on. The film remains controversial amongst Bond fans but, for many, the movie's shortcomings were compensated for by the return of Sean Connery as 007.

A View To A Kill (1985)

ROGER MOORE'S FINAL STINT AS 007 also marked the swansong of another regular – Lois Maxwell, who had played Moneypenny in every Bond movie so far. *A View To A Kill* was the second film in the series to eschew all traces of its source, an Ian Fleming short story *From A View To A Kill*. The

Irvin Kershner who helmed *The Empire Strikes Back* was selected. British comedy writers Dick Clement and Ian La Frenais were brought in, uncredited, to freshen up Lorenzo Semple Jr's script. Semple himself was best known for his work on the Sixties *Batman* television series.

The film is, inevitably, a re-make of *Thunderball* with some diversions and minor changes to character names. A middle-aged James Bond is plucked from semi-retirement by M and sent to a health farm where he discovers a SPECTRE plot to extort money from the production suffered budget cuts and Pinewood's 007 stage was destroyed in a fire in June 1984. Cubby Broccoli opted to rebuild it rather than relocate interior filming to Hollywood and the new stage was completed within four months. Meanwhile, Roger Moore made it known he was unhappy at the escalation of on screen violence and bloodshed during this film.

The screenplay, by the familiar team of Richard Maibaum and Michael G Wilson, aimed to refresh the franchise by keeping it topical. Bond is sent to investigate Zorin Industries, a computer chip manufacturer in California. He discovers that the head of the company, Max Zorin (Christopher Walken) plans to activate the San Andreas Fault, plunging Silicon Valley into the ocean and leaving him with a monopoly on computer chips. Bond defeats Zorin in a climactic battle atop San Francisco's Golden Gate Bridge.

Christopher Walken, gives a chilling performance as the psychopathic Zorin and chanteuse Grace Jones is equally effective as May Day. Former Charlie's Angel Tanya Roberts looks stunning as Stacey Sutton, but critics were unconvinced by her portrayal of a geologist. British actress Fiona Fullerton plays a

The Living Daylights	
Bond Film Number	Fifteen
Year released	1987
Starring	Timothy Dalton
Director	John Glen
Score	John Barry
Filmed In	Morocco, Gibraltar, USA, England, Austria, Pinewood Studios
Budget	$40,000,000
Box Office Gross	$192,200,000

RIGHT 1987, The official fifteenth James Bond movie: *The Living Daylights*

although Moore had given sterling service, the years were catching up with him.

The Living Daylights (1987)

TIMOTHY DALTON'S IMPACT AS James Bond was immediate, presenting a radically different interpretation of the character to Roger Moore. The new 007 was harder-edged and much closer to the character in Fleming's novels than any of his predecessors. Eon Productions again succeeded in reinvigorating the franchise by taking it back to its original source. The change delighted Bond devotees but puzzled movie-goers accustomed to the genial Moore in the title role.

The services of director John Glen were retained whilst the writing team of Richard Maibaum and co-producer Michael G Wilson based the opening of their screenplay on Fleming's eponymous short story, adding additional material. General Koskov (Jeroen Krabbe), a defecting Soviet, warns of a Russian plan to kill enemy spies but shortly afterwards is apparently recap-

KGB agent also on the trail of Zorin. She ends up in bed with Bond, part of the film's theme of détente which culminates in 007 being granted the Order of Lenin. *Avengers* star Patrick McNee, as MI6 agent Sir Godfrey Tibbett, enjoys great on-screen chemistry with Moore.

Audience and critical reaction to *A View To A Kill* was mixed with some commentators highlighting the gulf in ages between the elderly MI6 personnel – Moore was 57 – and their more youthful opposition. Box-office receipts were down on *Octopussy* and the rejuvenation of the series would continue into the next film;

tured by the KGB. Aided reluctantly by Koskov's jilted girlfriend (Maryam d'Abo) Kara Milovy, 007 discovers that the defection is a set-up and that Koskov, in tandem with arms dealer Brad Whitaker (Joe Don Baker) and henchman Necros (Andreas Wisniewski), plans to escalate tension between East and West to exploit the increased arms spending.

The Living Daylights portrayed 007's world as a much more serious and dangerous place. The reliance on juvenile comedy and sight gags was jettisoned; the film's lighter moments sprung from character, particularly Desmond Llewellyn's practised turn as Q, but some critics misinterpreted this as a lack of humour.

Bond was almost monogamous during the movie, partly through the demands of the story but also as a reflection of the worldwide concern over the threat of AIDS. 007 still smokes, drinks, gambles and drives too fast but his relationship with the new Miss Moneypenny (Caroline Bliss) is notable for a lack of flirtatiousness.

Box-office receipts were up on *A View To A Kill* but reviews were cautious – Dalton's performance was praised, although some critics compared him

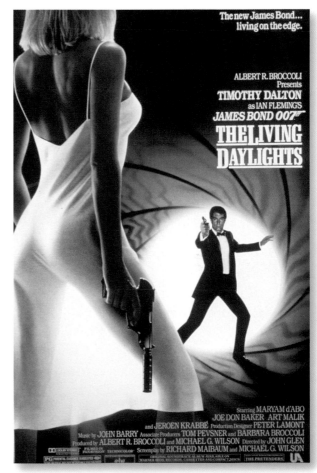

The new James Bond...
living on the edge.

ALBERT R. BROCCOLI
Presents
TIMOTHY DALTON
as IAN FLEMING'S
JAMES BOND 007
THE LIVING
DAYLIGHTS

Starring MARYAM d'ABO
JOE DON BAKER ART MALIK
and JEROEN KRABBÉ Production Designer PETER LAMONT
Music by JOHN BARRY Associate Producers TOM PEVSNER and BARBARA BROCCOLI
Produced by ALBERT R. BROCCOLI and MICHAEL G. WILSON Directed by JOHN GLEN
Screenplay by RICHARD MAIBAUM and MICHAEL G. WILSON

unfavourably to Connery and Moore. Perhaps the most damaging criticism of *The Living Daylights* was that it lacked a truly memorable villain. Nevertheless, Eon had proved that they could completely overhaul their hero and still thrive.

Licence To Kill (1989)

NOT SINCE *ON HER MAJESTY'S Secret Service* had a Bond film provoked such controversy amongst audiences

Licence To kill	
Bond Film Number	Sixteen
Year released	1989
Starring	Timothy Dalton
Director	John Glen
Score	Michael Kamen
Filmed In	Florida, Mexico
Budget	$42,000,000
Box Office Gross	$156,200,000

and critics. Taking the realism of *The Living Daylights* a step further, *Licence To Kill* plunged the series into previously uncharted territory. Timothy Dalton's second and final outing as Bond also proved the end of an era in other ways.

The movie was John Glen's swansong, after five consecutive pictures – more than any other 007 director. Robert Brown and Caroline Bliss signed off as M and Moneypenny respectively. Veteran screenwriter Richard Maibaum, now 80 years old, contributed his last script, in collaboration again with co-producer Michael G Wilson. *Licence To Kill* was the first official Bond movie not to take its title directly from an Ian Fleming novel or short story.

The screenplay sent Bond on a revenge mission after his old friend Felix Leiter – played by Richard Edison, recreating the role he first played in *Live And Let Die*, 16 years earlier – is kidnapped by drug baron Sanchez shortly after his wedding. Leiter's wife is murdered and he is horribly mutilated by a shark (a similar fate befell the character in the novel *Live And Let Die*). 007 goes rogue, having been denied M's permission to hunt down Sanchez. He is aided in his task by Pam Bouvier (Carey Lowell) an intrepid freelance pilot who occasionally works for the CIA.

Although *Licence To Kill* was regarded as a fine thriller, some critics felt that it was not really a Bond movie as it lacked several of the traditional elements and took itself too seriously. The climactic tanker lorry chase, overseen by associate producer Barbara Broccoli, was praised as exciting and suspenseful.

A late title change from *Licence Revoked*, because US audiences would not understand the word "revoked", led to a publicity campaign being scrapped and an ineffective substitute being used by MGM who compounded the felony by releasing the movie in direct competition with summer blockbusters *Raiders Of The Lost Ark*, *Lethal Weapon 2* and *Batman*. The fallout went further, embroiling Eon/Danjaq in litigation with MGM which would delay the next Bond movie for six years.

GoldenEye (1995)

IT WAS ALL CHANGE FOR THE return of 007, six years after his last appearance. Not only was there a new

GoldenEye	
Bond Film Number	Seventeen
Year released	1995
Starring	Pierce Brosnan
Director	Martin Campbell
Score	Eric Serra
Filmed In	Russia, Monte Carlo, The Caribbean, Switzerland, Puerto Rico, Leavesden Studios
Budget	$60,000,000
Box Office Gross	$353,400,000

RIGHT 1995, The official seventeenth James Bond movie: *Goldeneye*

Symbolic of these changes was the new, female M played by Dame Judi Dench who, in a pivotal scene, calls Bond a "sexist, misogynist dinosaur". A new Moneypenny, played by the aptly-named Samantha Bond, makes her debut. Amidst the new faces, Desmond Llewellyn's scene-stealing performance as Q provides continuity with the past.

The screenplay had been reworked by various hands and was ultimately credited to Jeffrey Caine and Bruce Feirstein from a story by Michael France. The film opens with Bond and 006 (Alec Trevelyan, played by Sean Bean) destroying a Soviet chemical weapons factory. Trevelyan is presumed killed whilst Bond escapes. Nine years later, Bond is investigating the theft of two nuclear GoldenEye satellites and is shocked to find that Trevelyan, who survived and became head of a Russian crime syndicate, is planning to use them to destroy the British economy.

Famke Janssen's gloriously over-the-top villainess Xenia Onatopp tends to overshadow Izabella Scorupco's intelligent performance as Natalya Simonova, a Bond girl who is not afraid to challenge the secret agent. 007's other allies included Joe Don Baker (previously a

actor as Bond, with Pierce Brosnan finally able to take on the role he was first offered in 1986, but Cubby Broccoli had passed day to day control of Eon Productions to his daughter Barbara and stepson Michael G Wilson. The outside world had altered too; the end of the Cold War and the dismantling of the Soviet Union raised serious doubts over the relevance of James Bond as a hero for the Nineties. Addressing this, *GoldenEye* presented 007 as essentially the same character facing up to the new world order.

villain in *The Living Daylights*) as CIA agent Jack Wade and Robbie Coltrane as Zukovsky, a Russian Mafioso who strikes up an uneasy alliance with Bond.

GoldenEye wowed the critics with its winning combination of new and old and shattered all previous box-office records for Bond movies.

Tomorrow Never Dies (1997)

THE EIGHTEENTH BOND FILM WAS made to a tight schedule as MGM/UA wanted it ready for Christmas 1997 and principal photography only began in April. The production ran into early difficulties; both Pinewood and the recently-built Leavesden facility were unavailable so Eon had to build another new studio in St Albans to accommodate the movie – although some scenes were shot at Pinewood. The Vietnamese government's eleventh-hour decision to withdraw permission to film in their country was overcome by using Thailand. Rumours from the set suggested that director Roger Spotiswoode and screenwriter Bruce Feirstein had

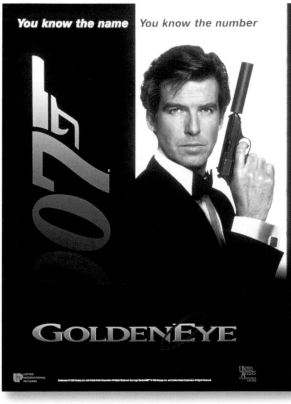

fallen out and that Pierce Brosnan and Teri Hatcher were not getting on.

Despite these setbacks, *Tomorrow Never Dies* was delivered on time and was hailed as a great 007 movie. Combining a contemporary feel with classic elements of Bond, the movie sees the secret agent pitted against a classic, megalomaniacal villain. Media magnate Elliot Carver (Jonathan Pryce) plans to create nuclear war between Britain and China to boost the ratings of his newspapers and cable TV channels. 007 teams up with Chinese agent Colonel Wai Lin (Michelle Yeoh) to prevent this.

Brosnan presents a leaner, fitter James Bond. The actor suffered a facial injury during shooting which meant that he could only be filmed from one side until

it healed. Leather cat-suited Yeoh, one of the Orient's biggest screen stars, was the latest Bond girl to resist 007 until the mission was over. The relationship between Judi Dench's M and 007 seems to have thawed a little since *GoldenEye* as she allows him more leeway.

More bad news arrived when it became apparent that *Tomorrow Never Dies* would be opening at the same time as James Cameron's *Titanic* and it was widely predicted that the Bond movie would sink at the box-office. Although the rival film went on to become a record-breaking blockbuster, *Tomorrow Never Dies* was a massive hit in itself, nearly as successful as *GoldenEye* worldwide whilst it outperformed its predecessor to become the top-earning Bond film in the vital American market.

The World Is Not Enough (1999)

LIKE MOORE AND CONNERY, PIERCE Brosnan's third outing as Bond saw him settle comfortably into the role of the secret agent, turning in an elegant and authoritative performance. *The World Is*

Tomorow Never Dies	
Bond Film Number	Eighteen
Year released	1997
Starring	Pierce Brosnan
Director	Roger Spotiswoode
Score	David Arnold
Filmed In	England, Hong Kong, Thailand, Pinewood Studios
Budget	$110,000,000
Box Office Gross	$346,6000,000

Not Enough continued the series' highly effective balancing act of presenting the familiar but avoiding formula by adding new elements.

First time Bond director Michael Apted had served an apprenticeship on British television in the Sixties; his CV included many episodes of *Coronation Street* but he was not known for action movies. Apted was well aware of the need to bring in fresh ideas and fashioned new twists to the ski chase and boat chase scenes. The screenplay, written by Neil Purvis and Robert Wade with Bruce Feirstein brought in to rework it, provided another innovation – for the first time in a 007 film, the main villain is female.

Elektra King (French actress Sophie Marceau) is the daughter of murdered oil magnate and friend of M, Sir Robert King. Bond is assigned to protect her from the psychopathic Renard (Robert Carlyle) who once kidnapped her. It transpires that Elektra killed her father and is working with Renard in a plan to detonate a nuclear device in a strategic oil pipeline, which 007, naturally, thwarts. Having earlier fallen for Elektra, Bond is forced to assassinate her.

The World Is Not Enough contains one

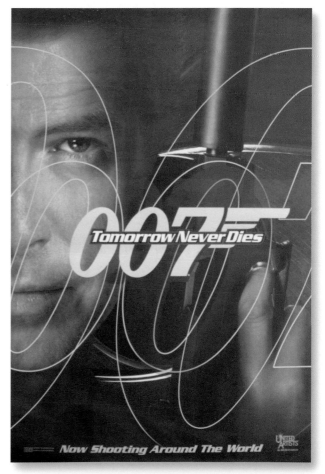

of the best casts of the series. Sophie Marceau exudes allure and evil alternately whilst Carlyle adds a layer of humanity to the villain's role. Dame Judi Dench returns as M and is given a more prominent role as she flies to Turkey where she is kidnapped by Elektra before helping Bond conclude the mission. Robbie Coltrane reprises his *GoldenEye* role as General Zukovsky, striking up another uneasy alliance with 007. Sadly, Desmond Llewellyn makes the last of 17 appearances as Q; the actor died in a car accident shortly after the premiere.

The World Is Not Enough saw Pierce Brosnan hailed as the billion-dollar Bond as the combined gross for his three movies exceeded that sum.

The World Is Not Enough	
Bond Film Number	Nineteen
Year released	1999
Starring	Pierce Brosnan
Director	Michael Apted
Score	David Arnold
Filmed In	Spain, England, Pinewood Studios
Budget	$135,000,000
Box Office Gross	$390,000,000

Die Another Day (2002)

THE BOND SERIES CELEBRATED ITS fortieth anniversary in 2002 with *Die Another Day*. The twentieth film is loaded with references to previous movies, serving as a reminder that Pierce Brosnan's 007 is the same character originally portrayed by Sean Connery. At the same time, James Bond is established as an icon for the 21st century. Of Maori descent, Lee Tamahori was a first-time Bond director whose work saw *Die Another Day* relying on CGI effects more than any of its predecessors. Neal Purvis and Robert Wade were invited back to write a screenplay which took Bond into unfamiliar territory.

In the pre-credits sequence, 007 is captured and tortured by North Korean troops after a mission to infiltrate a military base operated by Colonel Moon (Will Yun Lee). When he is released 14

LEFT Sophie Marceau during a press conference for the *The World is Not Enough*

months later, M suspends him fearing that he may have disclosed secret information under torture.

Determined to restore his reputation, Bond takes matters into his own hands, teaming up with American agent Jinx Johnson (Halle Berry) to discover that Colonel Moon has undergone gene therapy to change his appearance and has assumed the identity of British billionaire Gustav Graves (Toby Stephens). Graves plans to use a satellite weapon to reunite North and South Korea by destroying the minefield between them.

John Cleese is the new Q, and visual references to past gadgets abound in his scenes with Bond. Although uncredited, Madonna, who performed the title song, appears briefly on screen as a fencing instructor.

As so often happens with Bond films, *Die Another Day* divided the critics with some complaining that the use of CGI was excessive. 007's fencing scene with

Die Another Day	
Bond Film Number	Twenty
Year released	2002
Starring	Pierce Brosnan
Director	Lee Tamahori
Score	David Arnold
Filmed In	England, Spain, Iceland, Pinewood Studios
Budget	$142,000,000
Box Office Gross	$456,000,000

Graves was praised as one of the best fight sequences of the series and the ice palace compared favourably with classic sets of old.

Die Another Day was another box-office sensation, setting records for its opening weekends in both Britain and America. Although it was not apparent at the time of release, the movie would prove to be Pierce Brosnan's swansong as the secret agent.

Casino Royale (2006)

WITH ENGLISH ACTOR DANIEL Craig installed as the sixth James Bond, the franchise underwent arguably its most radical reinvention, taking the character back to when he was originally granted his "00" licence and following his first mission. The rights to Ian Fleming's novel had been finally acquired in 1999 and its basic story was retained. Neal Purvis, Robert Wade and Paul Haggis wrote the screenplay and Martin Campbell, who helmed Pierce Brosnan's debut in *GoldenEye*, returned as director.

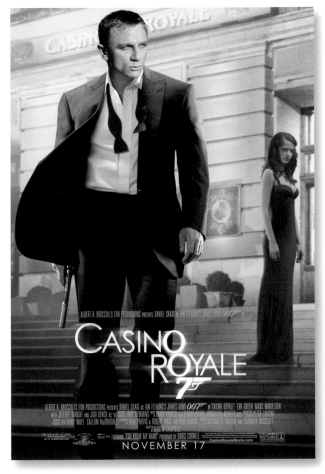

Quantum Of Solace (2008)

TAKING ITS NAME FROM AN IAN Fleming short story, *Quantum Of Solace* is the twenty-second official Bond movie. Its shooting schedule was extended by six months when director Roger Mitchell dropped out to be replaced by German-Swiss filmmaker Marc Forster. Long-term production designer Peter Lamont retired after 18 Bonds and was succeeded by Dennis

Glassner, whose work drew favourable comparisons with Ken Adam. The *Casino Royale* writing team of Paul Haggis, Robert Wade and Neal Purvis was augmented by Joshua Zetumer.

Uniquely for a 007 film, *Quantum Of Solace* carries on directly from its predecessor, taking its hero on a psychological journey. Still headstrong, Bond wants revenge for the death of Vesper Lynd. He is on the trail of Dominic Greene (acclaimed French actor Mathieu Amalric), leader of the terrorist organisation Quantum.

Bond discovers a connection between Greene and Vesper. Using an environmental organisation as cover, Greene plans to overthrow the government of Bolivia. Along the way, Bond encounters the enigmatic Camille (played by Ukrainian actress and model Olga Kurylenko), a Russian-Bolivian agent with personal reasons for pursuing Greene.

Much of the supporting cast from *Casino Royale* return including Judi Dench as M, Giancarlo Giannini as Rene Mathis and Jeffrey Wright, who becomes only the second actor after David Hedison to play Bond's American ally Felix Leiter twice. Jesper Christensen's deadly Mr White is back

Quantum Of Solace	
Bond Film Number	Twenty Two
Year released	2008
Starring	Daniel Craig
Director	Marc Forster
Score	David Arnold
Filmed In	Panama, Chile, Austria, Pinewood Studios
Budget	$113,400,000
Box Office Gross	Released 2008

whilst Gemma Arterton debuts as Agent Fields, whose appearance is partly an homage to earlier Bond girls such as Diana Rigg and Honor Blackman.

Filming was eventful. In addition to an injury to Daniel Craig's ribs, thank-fully not serious, an Aston Martin plunged into Lake Garda while two stuntmen were hospitalised, one in intensive care, after an accident during the filming of a chase sequence.

James Bond will return in 2010…

Chapter 5

The Cars

RIGHT The Aston Martin DB5 from *Goldfinger*

YOU ARE WHAT YOU DRIVE AND 007 has never been short of a stylish set of wheels…with one or two non-standard surprises.

Before the celebrated Aston Martin DB5 made its debut in *Goldfinger*, James Bond was seen behind the wheel of a more modest Sunbeam Alpine in *Dr No*, whilst in the novels he originally owned a Bentley. This was replaced in the literary *Goldfinger* by an Aston Martin DB III (in reality a model used for racing) which possessed rudimentary gadgets – a hidden compartment and tracking device – that formed the basis for Q's more extravagant adaptations in the movie.

The DB5 was a pricey, exclusive two-door coupe sports car – so expensive that the film's budget would not stretch to buying one! So Aston Martin loaned the vehicle to Eon and subsequently used it for promotional purposes. Its array of deadly extras, most of which were used in the chase sequence, included machine guns behind the front indicators, a revolving tyre slasher, a rear smoke screen, an ejector seat and a bullet-proof windscreen. The follow-up, *Thunderball*, featured mainly aquatic action, but the popularity of the DB5 was such that it reappeared in the movie's pre-title sequence when a new weapon, a water cannon, allowed 007 to wash away his pursuers. The car can also be spotted briefly later in the film.

Opportunities for product placement and merchandising meant that Bond would be seen behind the wheel of other makes, but the Aston Martin became part of the iconography of the series and was often used as a continuity device when a new 007 was cast. During *On Her Majesty's Secret Service* George Lazenby drove a brand-new DBS model

4711 · EA · 62

RIGHT Barbara Bach
and Roger Moore,
stars of *The Spy Who
Loved Me* pictured with
the 'amphibious'
Lotus Esprit

which had a telescopic rifle built into the glove compartment. Timothy Dalton was also given a pristine Aston Martin for *The Living Daylights*. His V8 was a high-performance supercar and came equipped with laser beams, spiked tyres, bullet-proof windows, rockets and a self-destruct function.

Pierce Brosnan's Bond kept a vintage 1964 DB5 for personal use in *GoldenEye*, and this was also seen fleetingly in *Tomorrow Never Dies*. Its most significant adaptation was a refrigerated compartment containing a bottle of Bollinger champagne. The Aston Martin Vanquish from *Die Another Day* had perhaps the most outlandish gimmick – "adaptive camouflage" which allowed it to effectively become invisible. Daniel Craig's 007 won an Aston Martin in a game of poker in *Casino Royale*. During the making of *Quantum Of Solace* in 2008, a stunt driver lost control of a DBS V12 (an updated version of the DB5) in difficult conditions and it ended up in an Italian lake.

Sean Connery was closely associated with two cars which actually belonged to his female companions. The most famous Bond car not actually driven by 007 was *You Only Live Twice*'s Toyota

ABOVE Aston Martin Vanquish from *Casino Royale*

RIGHT Jaguar XK-R as used by Bond villain Zao in *Die Another Day*

2000 GT, the driver's seat being occupied by Japanese agent Aki. Toyota did not actually make a convertible model; the version seen in the movie was specially manufactured. One of the highlights of *Diamonds Are Forever* was the spectacularly destructive car chase through Las Vegas where Bond tilted Tiffany Case's Ford Mustang Mach 1 on two wheels through an alleyway to evade pursuing police.

Roger Moore deliberately steered clear of the accoutrements of Connery's Bond and was the only screen 007 not to drive an Aston Martin. The first spectacular car stunt of Moore's tenure was performed in an AMC (American Motor Company) Hornet Hatchback which completed a

360° turn in mid-air after Bond appropriated it from a dealership in *The Man With The Golden Gun*.

The classic Moore-era vehicle was the submersible Lotus Esprit which made a splash in *The Spy Who Loved Me*. Apparently indestructible, the heavily-armed car became amphibious at the flick of a switch. In reality six different cars, including models, were required

ABOVE Citroen 2CV as featured in Bond film *For Your Eyes Only*

RIGHT BMW Z8 used in Bond movie *The World Is Not Enough*

for the transformation. A return was inevitable and *For Your Eyes Only* featured two Lotuses. The first explodes when a thug tries to steal it, whilst the second has no gadgetry but is massively turbocharged, capable of achieving 0-150mph in 15 seconds. In comic contrast, the film features perhaps the most unlikely Bond car chase with 007 in a Citroen 2CV driven by Melinda Havelock.

BMW established itself as a major supplier of motor vehicles to MI6 during Pierce Brosnan's time as Bond. The German company's Z3 Roadster, Bond's business car, appeared in *GoldenEye* several months before it was available to buy. None of the gadgets described by Q – ejec-

tor seat, parachute braking system and missiles – are actually used in the movie.

There were no such disappointments in the car chase in *Tomorrow Never Dies* where the BMW 750iL used most of its formidable arsenal and Bond employed its most ingenious feature, driving by remote control via an Ericsson mobile phone. The company's three-film product placement deal ended with *The World Is Not Enough* where their newest model, the immensely powerful Z8, was showcased before being sawn in half by a rotating blade suspended from a helicopter.

Whatever lies in the future, if James Bond drives it then you can be sure it'll be the wheel deal!

Chapter 6

The Gadgets

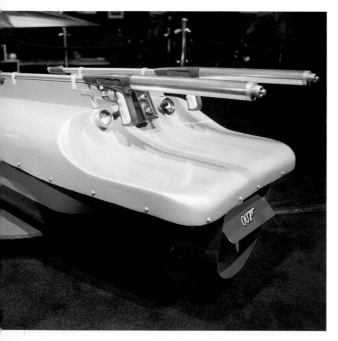

BOND HAS ALWAYS BEEN AT THE forefront of technology, with devices to get him out of the tightest corner.

Desmond Llewellyn made his debut as Major Boothroyd, supplier of 007's gadgetry, in From Russia With Love: the name Q came later. The deadly attaché case, an exaggerated version of the one described in the novel, was a relatively modest and believable start to the series' fascination with gadgets. Here it is, along with some of its more memorable if sometimes far-fetched successors.

Glass Shattering Ring
(Die Another Day)

An unremarkable piece of finger jewellery transforms into an "ultra high-frequency single-digit sonic agitator unit" that can shatter bullet-proof glass.

Gyrocopter
(You Only Live Twice)

A mini helicopter named "Little Nellie" armed with machine guns, rocket launchers, heat-seeking missiles and mines gave Bond the flight of his life.

Camera Gun *(Licence To Kill)*

Timothy Dalton's Bond joined the paparazzi with a camera that converts into a sniper rifle and can be fired by him alone. Unfortunately his aim proved less impressive!

Attaché Case
(From Russia With Love)

Ammo, a knife that projects from the side, 50 gold sovereigns in the lining and a bottle of tear gas marked talcum powder, this is indeed, as M puts it, "A smart-looking piece of luggage".

Jet-pack *(Thunderball)*

After killing Colonel Douvar in the opening sequence of 1965's *Thunderball*, Bond (Sean Connery) spectacularly escapes retribution by taking off from a balcony in a jet-pack.

Electromagnetic Watch
(Live And Let Die)

Moneypenny gave Roger Moore's Bond a Rolex Submariner with a powerful electromagnet that, Q claims, can deflect a bullet. Its spinning bezel let him cut his ropes and escape a pool full of sharks.

ABOVE Pierce Brosnan modelling the Omega Seamaster watch

LEFT The Underwater Tow Sled, as used in *Thunderball*

ABOVE Little Nelly

RIGHT Volcano owned by the criminal syndicate SPECTRE built for *You Only Live Twice*

Laser Watch *(GoldenEye)*

When Bond (Pierce Brosnan) and Natalya Simonova are locked in a train that's set to explode, his Omega Seamaster Pro cuts a hole in the carriage floor with a laser beam.

Cellphone
(Tomorrow Never Dies)

No ordinary mobile for Bond, this Sony Ericsson number incorporates a stun gun, a fingerprint analyser and can also be used to pick locks.

Jet-ski
(The Spy Who Loved Me)

Kawasaki had only just started mass producing the jet-ski in 1976, so Bond's spectacular use of one in the movie single-handedly launched the personal watercraft industry.

Exploding Toothpaste
(Licence To Kill)

Plastic explosives disguised as ordinary toothpaste that picks up the detonation signal from a transmitter disguised as a packet of cigarettes. Hazardous to health!

Chapter 7

Villains

RIGHT The menacing Blofeld played by Donald Pleasance stroking his cat

WHEN IT COMES TO BOND MOVIES, the gadgets and the girls, even the cars, have to play second fiddle to the villains.

Everything else is just window dressing if Bond can't overcome his adversaries and save the day. And some very willing villains have pitted their wits and wiles against our man from MI6 over the years. Most are one-offs, while one in particular stayed the course in style, but all have been in their own way memorable.

After the eponymous *Dr No* fought Bond and lost in the first movie, *From Russia With Love* unveiled Bond's longest-lived opponent. Perhaps unveiled is the wrong word. Ernst Stavro Blofeld, the white cat-loving mastermind of SPECTRE, was referred to only as "number one"; his face remained unseen and his name was not revealed until the closing credits.

Returning after a movie's break in *Thunderball*, Blofeld's face again remained tantalisingly hidden; he was once more portrayed by Anthony Dawson and voiced by Eric Pohlmann. Then, in *You Only Live Twice*, in which Sean Connery's Bond had to evade Blofeld's deadly pool of piranha fish, Blofeld's face was revealed at last. The villain was portrayed by veteran British character actor Donald Pleasance for the only time, while a pre-Kojak Telly Savalas was required to take a more physical approach than his predecessors as Blofeld in *On Her Majesty's Secret Service*.

1971's *Diamonds Are Forever* marked Blofeld's final appearance as the major villain in a Bond movie. Again played by a British actor, Charles Grey, the character had changed his appearance (presumably by plastic surgery) and grown a

full head of hair! He would, however, crop up just once more in the non-authorised *Never Say Never Again*, in which he was portrayed by Max Von Sydow. The return of Sean Connery clearly demanded a reprise from Bond's most dogged adversary.

Oddjob, the henchman of Auric Goldfinger in – what else? – *Goldfinger* was Bond's first supernaturally strong foe, assisted by karate skills and a hard hat. This paved the way for the 7' tall Richard Kiel as Jaws, the seemingly indestructible assassin with razor-sharp steel teeth who was such a hit with movie-goers, children in particular, when he turned up in *The Spy Who Loved Me* that he would secure an invitation to return.

Moving into the 80s, *Octopussy* featured two top-notch foes in Stephen Berkoff, perfectly cast as the insane General Orlov, and Louis Jordan's urbane, suave and treacherous Khan – an archetypal Bond villain. 007 could have met a famous face, however, had David Bowie and Sting not turned down the role of the psychopathic Zorin in *A View To A Kill.* As it turned out Christopher

LEFT "You expect me to talk?" Goldfinger: "No, Mr Bond, I expect you to die."

Walken acquitted himself well, assisted by singer Grace Jones as his Amazonian girlfriend May Day. Unscrupulous drugs baron Franz Sanchez, played by Robert Davi, will go down in infamy for maiming Felix Leiter, Bond's pal of some 16 years standing, in *Licence To Kill*. Indeed, the shock was enough to send Bond off

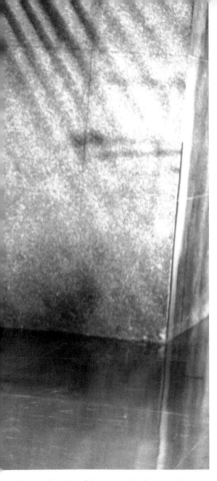

Sean Bean. Trevelyan was 006 who comes back from the dead to leap the Iron Curtain and join the "other side". But even more memorable was his hench-woman Xenia Onatopp, played by Famke Janssen, who kills men by squeezing them with her thighs!

Another well-known young British actor, Robert Carlyle, took on a villain-ous role in *The World Is Not Enough*. His character Renard was impervious to all sensation because of a bullet lodged in his brain, which allowed for all kinds of nasty fun and games.

By 2002 and *Die Another Day*, the vil-lain changed from oriental to occidental during the course of the movie, thanks to the miracle of plastic surgery – and while Toby Stephens as Gustav Graves was a dab hand with a blade, it wasn't a tactic likely to create empathy with the character as in days of old.

Chiselled Dane Mads Mikkelsen gave the blood-weeping Le Chiffre a chilling air of menace from across the gaming table as Daniel Craig's first adversary in *Casino Royale* and we now await the next man (or woman) to take on James Bond. Who knows – as we've travelled back in time, it could be time for Blofeld (and his feline friend) to take an encore!

LEFT Bond and Oddjob fight in the film *Goldfinger*

the rails. But his next challenge, having had his licence to kill restored, saw him up against one of his own – Alec Trevelyan, played by a familiar face in

Chapter 8

Themes and Songs

RIGHT Matt Monro
sang the theme tune
From Russia with Love

BOND SONGS HAVE TRADITIONally been both in tune with the times and timeless – like the man himself.

Few pieces of music have captured the essence of a character as successfully as *The James Bond Theme*. Composed by former big-band singer Monty Norman as part of his Dr No soundtrack, John Barry's pulsating arrangement was used for the opening credits. The John Barry Seven had enjoyed several hits and the group's guitarist Vic Flick played the famous guitar figure. When, in 2001, Norman sued the *Sunday Times* for libel after it suggested that Barry wrote the theme, the court ruled that Norman was sole composer.

The first of John Barry's 11 Bond scores was *From Russia With Love*. He established himself as the definitive 007 composer with *Goldfinger* by using a winning combination of brass, jazz and exotic melodies. Barry's last Bond score was 1987's *The Living Daylights,* but his influence endured in the work of David Arnold who has scored every 007 movie since *Tomorrow Never Dies*. Arnold's 1997 album of new versions of Bond music, *Shaken Not Stirred,* met with Barry's approval and he nominated Arnold as his successor.

In the absence of a title song from *Dr No*, the John Barry Orchestra's version of *The James Bond Theme* was a Number 13 hit in 1962 (a remix by Moby from *Tomorrow Never Dies* peaked at 8 in 1997). Matt Munro crooned *From Russia With Love* which was followed by Shirley Bassey belting out *Goldfinger*. The ultimate Bond diva also sang *Diamonds Are Forever* and *Moonraker*, making her a record-breaking three-time Bond singer.

RIGHT John Barry wrote the score to several Bond films

Nancy Sinatra's *You Only Live Twice* reached Number 11 in 1967 and a sample from the song featured in Robbie Williams' chart-topper *Millennium* in 1998. Tom Jones gave his all on *Thunderball,* but the song failed to chart. *On Her Majesty's Secret Service* saw Barry opting for an instrumental main theme. *We Have All the Time In The World*, with lyrics by Hal David and sung by Louis Armstrong, finally became a top three hit when used in a Guinness television advertisement in 1994.

A new era for Bond began in 1973 with *Live And Let Die* when Paul McCartney wrote (with wife Linda) and sang the dramatic title piece which reunited him with soundtrack composer George Martin for the first time since the Beatles' split. The song went top 10 on both sides of the Atlantic. Barry's return for *The Man With The Golden Gun* was undistinguished, as was Lulu's rendition of his theme song.

In contrast, *Nobody Does It Better* from *The Spy Who Loved Me* was a classic Bond number. Written by Marvin Hamlisch and Carole Bayer Sager and performed by Carly Simon, it proved the series' biggest transatlantic hit so far. With John Barry unavailable to work in

Britain because of tax reasons, Hamlisch's score included a disco version of the main theme, *Bond '77*.

After Blondie's proposed title song *For Your Eyes Only* (1981) was rejected, Sheena Easton performed Bill Conti and Michael Leeson's ditty over the movie's opening titles, a privilege unique in Bond films. Conti supplied the pop and disco-inflected score.

Octopussy (1983) ranked as one of Fleming's least song-friendly titles and not even the return of Barry, with lyricist Tim Rice, could help Rita Coolidge's *All Time High* to rise beyond Number 75 in Britain.

David Bowie and Sting might have declined the part of villain Max Zorin in *A View To A Kill* but pop sensations Duran Duran performed the theme tune, a collaboration between Barry and the band, and were rewarded with the biggest Bond hit, a UK Number 2 and US Number 1.

In an attempt to recreate this success, Norwegian heart-throbs A-ha performed *The Living Daylights* and reached Number 5 in the UK. The movie also contains two songs by the Pretenders – *If There Was A Man* (over the end credits) and *Where Has*

LEFT Three-time Bond Chanteuse Shirley Bassey

RIGHT Duran Duran have had the most commercially successful Bond song with *A View To A Kill*

Everybody Gone (on villain Necros' Walkman). Guitar legends Eric Clapton and Vic Flick were approached to provide music for *Licence To Kill* (1989), but when that fell through Gladys Knight performed the title piece which was based on the horn theme from *Goldfinger*. *Robin Hood* man Michael Kamen stepped into Barry's shoes for the soundtrack.

French avant-garde composer Eric Serra's experimental score for *GoldenEye* was condemned by the critics as inappropriate for a Bond movie. Written by U2's Bono and the Edge and sung by Tina Turner, the theme tune might have looked a winner on paper but proved unpopular with 007 fans.

For *Tomorrow Never Dies* (1997) the main song was chosen after a competitive process involving 12 artists, Sheryl Crow emerging triumphant. Disappointed entrants included Marc Almond, Saint Etienne and Pulp. David Arnold wrote *The World Is Not Enough* with lyricist Don Black which was performed by Garbage. Black had previously collaborated with John Barry on *Thunderball*, *Diamonds Are Forever* and *The Man With The Golden Gun*. Arnold had intended

that *Only Myself To Blame*, sung by Scott Walker, would feature over the closing titles, but it was ultimately replaced by a techno version of *The James Bond Theme*.

Securing the services of Madonna to

write and sing the theme tune for 2002's *Die Another Day* was a coup for the producers. The approach changed again for *Casino Royale* with Chris Cornell, lead singer of Audioslave and Soundgarden, performing *You Know My Name*, co-written with David Arnold. This was the first piece to open and close a Bond movie since 1985's *A View To A Kill* and the first by a male vocalist since 1987.

Chapter 9

Collectables

RIGHT The Airfix model
of the James Bond
Aston Martin DB5

BOND'S SPIN-OFF TOYS AND SOU-venirs have become sought-after in their own right.

The earliest Bond movie collectables were the soundtrack records and original film posters. Some *From Russia With Love* memorabilia – a replica attaché case (without tear-gas spray!), jigsaw puzzle and slide viewer – was issued, but only after the *Goldfinger*-inspired merchandising spree.

Corgi Toy's die-cast model of 007's Aston Martin DB5, first seen in *Goldfinger*, has been reissued and updated many times, selling over seven million copies. It was initially painted gold rather than the film's silver because Corgi felt it might look unfinished. As with all vintage toys, the original, boxed and in mint condition is the Holy Grail for collectors. The Corgi replica of the Toyota 2000 GT from *You Only Live*

Twice featured an extra not seen in the movie – a rocket launcher in the boot.

On Her Majesty's Secret Service produced few items of interest to collectors other than some cars in the Corgi Rockets range which are particularly scarce in boxed gift-set form. The company also made a replica of the moon buggy from *Diamonds Are Forever*.

Corgi's association with Bond continued with a die-cast version of amphibious Lotus Esprit from *The Spy Who Loved Me*, their second biggest seller. Along with other vehicles from the film, the Lotus was available in miniature Corgi Junior form, both separately and as part of a set. Similarly, Drax's helicopters and space shuttle from *Moonraker* appeared in full-size and Junior versions. Corgi's next Bond vehicle was the less exciting yellow Citroen 2CV featured in *For Your Eyes Only*.

Rival toy car firm Matchbox took over for *A View To A Kill*.

As well as their version of the Aston Martin, plastic kit manufacturers Airfix offered a boxed set of figures of 007 and Oddjob. Original unmade Airfix kits of the Toyota and the autogyro "Little Nellie" from *You Only Live Twice* are highly-prized items. Revell's *Moonraker* space shuttle kit is less popular.

American company Gilbert issued an action figure of Oddjob which is harder to find than the accompanying Bond doll. The 007 toy was reissued and updated with underwater apparatus to coincide with *Thunderball* in 1966. The Gilbert-produced *Thunderball* tie-in 007 Road Race Set, similar to Scalextric, is very scarce after being withdrawn due to a fault.

Several 007 board games were produced in the Sixties. The best was the finely-detailed *Thunderball*-based Largo v James Bond Underwater Battle, made by Triang of Hampshire.

British company Lone Star Toys marketed a James Bond Super Action Set comprising essential items for young spies, a grenade, gun and walkie-talkie. Lone Star reissued their standard 007 toy pistol in gold to tie in with *The Man With The Golden Gun*. The company were responsible for the replica guns from *A View To A Kill*. Also of interest to collectors is their cap-firing replica of Bond's *Moonraker* laser gun.

Of the various 007-related bubblegum cards, the most collectable is a set based on *Goldfinger* which was withdrawn in Britain for featuring too many bikini-clad women! Perhaps the rarest piece of Bond memorabilia from the Sixties is a French play set based on Blofeld's volcano headquarters.

The scarcest Bond comic is an adaptation of *Dr No* published by DC Comics in *Showcase* #43 in April 1963. There was then a long gap before Marvel Comics' productions of *For Your Eyes Only* and *Octopussy*. Subsequently,

Eclipse, Dark Horse and Topps have produced occasional movie adaptations, although none have appeared since the latter's *GoldenEye*.

For those with very deep pockets, first editions of Ian Fleming's novels have fetched over £20,000 whilst Ursula Andress' iconic white bikini from *Dr No* sold for £35,000 at auction in 1998. If you're shaken and stirred by the prices, search your attic for Bond treasure!

LEFT British Royal mail set of stamps to commemorate the centenary of the birth of Ian Fleming

BELOW James Bond Corgi DB5

Chapter 10

Iconography

BOND'S CINEMATIC INNOVATIONS have been much copied, not to mention parodied. Here are some famous and quirky examples.

Gun barrel sequence

MUCH OF THE ICONOGRAPHY OF James Bond was established in *Dr No*. This began with the "gun barrel sequence", the brainchild of titles designer Maurice Binder, a New Yorker who had been working in the British film industry since the 1950s. Binder had to come up with ideas for the sequence in just 15 minutes before a conference. Almost inseparable from the *James Bond Theme*, it opened every Bond movie until 2006's *Casino Royale*.

The scrolling white dots resemble gun-fire before the point of view switches to the interior of a gun. Bond strides into its sights, turns shoots then blood starts to seep down. Filming was accomplished by putting a pinhole camera into the barrel of a gun.

Dancing girls in opening titles

MAURICE BINDER ALSO DESIGNED the main titles and *Dr No* inaugurated a long tradition of featuring dancing girls against various backgrounds and projections. Because of a dispute with Eon, Binder was replaced by his assistant Robert Brownjohn for *From Russia With Love* and *Goldfinger* but the opening credits continued in the same vein in his absence. Returning with *Thunderball*, Binder worked on every subsequent Bond up to and including *Licence To Kill*. He died in 1991, Daniel Kleinman succeeding him as titles designer from *GoldenEye* onwards. *Casino Royale* finally broke the dancing girls tradition, its opening titles featuring Daniel Craig fighting against playing-card motifs.

ABOVE Girls feature strongly in the opening titles of the Bond movies

on "007". When *Goldfinger* was released, the image standardised to the now-familiar one of the gun adjacent to the "7" and pointing to the right. The design has remained constant, with slight variations, ever since.

The tuxedo

WHEN THE AUDIENCE FIRST SAW Bond, he was dressed in a black single-breasted shawl-collared dinner suit with white two-fold shirt and black bow tie. This classic piece of formal menswear has become synonymous with the character to the extent that it is the standard 007 fancy-dress costume!

The guns

THE CINEMATIC BOND HAS USED many firearms, the first and most iconic being the Walther PPK. This semi-automatic pistol was originally manufactured in Germany and used by the Nazis in World War II. The PPK was featured in almost every movie until *The World Is Not Enough*, when it was upgraded to a more modern Walther P99.

The 007 logo

ABOVE 007s Walther PPK

RIGHT Daniel Craig in black tuxedo

DESIGNED BY AMERICAN GRAPHIC artist Joseph Caroff for the British film poster for *Dr No*, the logo originally featured a gun and falling bullets overlaid

Chapter 11

Quotes

A selection of "Bond Mots", from Connery to Craig

"The target of my books lies somewhere between the solar plexus and the upper thigh." **Ian Fleming**

"Bond is a unique hero. There's none of this rubbish about I won't pull my gun until three seconds after he's pulled his. We try to keep the character of Bond as a hard, sometimes cruel man in the films. You might even call it 'sadism for the family'." **Cubby Broccoli**

"*Dr No* is the headiest box-office concoction of sex and sadism ever brewed in a British studio, strictly bath-tub hooch but a brutally potent intoxicant for all that." **Richard Whitehall, *Films and Filming***

"*From Russia With Love* is my favourite Bond film. I liked the story very much and I think it has more credibility than *Goldfinger* or *Thunderball*, which were quite fantastic. As the films got bigger and more expensive they became more involved with hardware and less involved with people." **Sean Connery**

"James Bond is the invincible figure every man would like to be, every woman is excited by and is everyone's survival symbol." **Sean Connery**

"I tell you, it's a mystery. All I did was wear this bikini in *Dr No*, not even a small one, and whoosh! Overnight, I made it." **Ursula Andress**

RIGHT Jack Lord hold's Sean Connery at gunpoint in *Dr. No*

"It wasn't easy to find another Ursula. I only wish I could." **Cubby Broccoli**

"Once you are a Bond girl, you are a Bond girl for life." **Claudine Auger**

"After all those well-equipped ladies, I was a bit of a surprise, wasn't I? I mean I'm not exactly all teeth and tits, am I?" **Diana Rigg**

"However many naked girls you think you see, if you look carefully you'll see that none of them are naked. And however many girls Bond gets into bed with, he only manages to have one kiss then something terrible happens." **Britt Ekland**

"The real drawback to acting Bond is that it's not acting. You are just a comic-strip hero, the central character around which the action and the gadgets revolve. Bond is exactly the same in the last scene as he is in the first. I'm not saying I'm the world's greatest actor, far from it, but I *do* enjoy acting." **Roger Moore**

"My only grumble about Bond films is that they don't tax one as an actor. All one really needs is the constitution of a rugby player to get through 18 weeks of swimming, slugging and necking."
Sean Connery

"I played Bond differently from Sean, a little lighter, a little more tongue-in-cheek. Maybe if Sean had continued after the first six, he'd have sent it up too." **Roger Moore**

"As a boy in 1964 after leaving Ireland, it was the first film I ever saw in London and it was unbelievable. A naked lady covered in gold paint. Oddjob with that hat. It was just magic. Sheer sophistication. Life changed for me." **Pierce Brosnan on** *Goldfinger*

"In a Bond film, you aren't involved in *cinema verite* or *avant-garde*. One is involved in colossal fun."
Terence Young, director

"I think what turned the Bond pictures around … was that car in *Goldfinger*. I think that the minute Sean pressed the button on the ejector seat, and the audience roared, the series turned around. The audiences saw outlandish things they had never seen before and the natural response of anybody – a writer or a filmmaker – is to give them what they want."
Tom Manciewicz, screenwriter

"Although I had been offered a contract for another film, I refused to sign it. I thought I knew better. I thought I could make my name with the film and then be taken up by other producers. And that way, I wouldn't get locked into the Bond image. Well, it was a crazy decision." **George Lazenby**

"Choose your next witticism carefully Mr Bond, it may be your last."
Auric Goldfinger

Bond: "Who would pay $1m to have me killed?" M: "Jealous husbands, outraged chefs, humiliated tailors … the list is endless." *The Man With The Golden Gun*

"There's a useful four letter word – and you're full of it." **Bond to Scaramanga in** *The Man With The Golden Gun*

"Farewell, Mr Bond. That word has, I must admit, a welcome ring of permanence about it." **Stromberg –** *The Spy Who Loved Me*

"Look after Mr Bond. See that some harm comes to him."
Hugo Drax – *Moonraker*

Admiral Roebuck: "With all due respect M, sometimes, I don't think you've got the balls for this job."
M (Judi Dench): "Perhaps but the advantage is that I don't have to think with them all the time." ***Tomorrow Never Dies***

"One day I saw Pierce holding that gun, I felt a weight falling away from my body. Only then I realised I'm back to being myself again, free." **Timothy Dalton**

"In 1986, I think I was 33 or something like that, and I still looked like a baby. Finally I'm growing into this face of mine. That takes time." **Pierce Brosnan**

"Sean Connery set and defined the character. He did something extraordinary with that role. He was bad, sexy, animalistic and stylish and it is because of him I am here today. I wanted Sean Connery's approval and he sent me messages of support which meant a lot to me." **Daniel Craig**

"Pierce and I had a few drinks over it and we discussed it. And his advice to me was, 'Go for it!' which I think is the best advice I could have got." **Daniel Craig**

Chapter 12

The Broccoli Dynasty

ALBERT "CUBBY" BROCCOLI WAS born on 5 April 1909, the eldest son of an Italian-American family living in Long Island, New York. Moving to Hollywood before the war, his career began as a third assistant director for Twentieth Century Fox, graduating to assistant director and working in that capacity on Howard Hughes' *The Outlaw*.

After serving in the United States Navy during the war, Broccoli moved to London in 1951. Taking advantage of the UK government's provision of subsidies for movies with British casts, he formed Warwick Films with Irving Allen. Broccoli's third marriage was to actress and novelist Dana Wilson. Dana's teenage son, Michael G Wilson, was to become a pivotal figure in Bond productions as did the couple's daughter Barbara, born in 1960.

Warwick Films made nearly 20 suc-cessful pictures but the company ran into financial difficulties, forcing Broccoli and Allen to fund *The Trials of Oscar Wilde* personally. The film drew ecstatic reviews but ran into censorship problems in America and, when Broccoli refused to make any cuts, was denied general release. The fallout brought down Warwick, leaving Broccoli on the verge of bankruptcy.

Broccoli became interested in pro-ducing a film based on Ian Fleming's work and discovered that the option on the rights to the James Bond novels was held by Harry Saltzman. An expatriate Canadian born in October 1925, Saltzman came to Britain in 1957 and formed Woodfall Films which spe-cialised in "kitchen sink" dramas like *Look Back In Anger* and *Saturday Night And Sunday Morning*. Broccoli was reluctant to form another partnership

BELOW Harry Saltzman and Albert Broccoli on the set of *You Only Live Twice*

RIGHT Barbara Broccoli has carried on where her father left off

but Saltzman refused to sell the option, so they created two companies – Eon Productions to make the films and Danjaq to hold the rights. Overcoming initial reluctance on the part of American studios, they secured a $1 million deal with United Artists to fund *Dr No*.

The two men were very different characters – Broccoli was purposeful and centred, Saltzman unpredictable and tempestuous, but the partnership endured for 15 years and nine Bond movies. During that time, Broccoli had only produced two non-007 films but Saltzman maintained many outside interests, including the Michael Caine Harry Palmer movies. These side ventures were a bone of contention but it was Saltzman's financial troubles that eventually fractured the partnership.

Now a lawyer, Michael G Wilson was able to guide his stepfather through the legal minefield of Saltzman's departure which was formalised in December 1975. Having made cameo appearances in several Bond pictures, he became actively involved in Eon Productions. Beginning as assistant to the producer on *The Spy Who Loved Me*, Wilson was executive producer for the next three movies before being credited as co-producer with Cubby Broccoli on *A View To A Kill*. He also collaborated with Richard Maibaum on many screenplays.

Health problems meant that *GoldenEye* was the last Bond that Cubby was actively involved in. After undergoing triple heart by-pass surgery, he died of heart failure on 27 June 1996, aged 87. Amongst his proudest achievements was receiving the prestigious Irving G Thalberg Award for creative producers, presented to him by Roger Moore at the 1981 Oscars.

Since the death of her father, Barbara Broccoli has co-produced the Bond films with Wilson, from *GoldenEye* onwards. She graduated from the Loyola University in Los Angeles with a degree in motion-picture and television communications and served as assistant director on *Octopussy* and *A View To A Kill* and as associate producer on *The Living Daylights* and *Licence To Kill*.

Both she and Wilson were awarded OBEs in 2008, confirming them as worthy inheritors of the dynasty.

007 Trivia

THE FIRST ACTOR TO PLAY JAMES Bond was American actor Barry Nelson in a 1954 television adaptation of *Casino Royale*.

The second actor to play James Bond was *Blockbuster* host Bob Holness in a South African radio production of *Moonraker* in 1956.

The Bond family motto, devised in the novel *On Her Majesty's Secret Service*, is "The World Is Not Enough", later the title of the 1999 film.

Colonel Sun by Robert Markham (Kingsley Amis) was the only non-Fleming Bond novel to be adapted to be adapted as a *Daily Express* comic-strip serial.

The first non-Fleming Bond novel to be licensed by copyright holders Glidrose was 1967's *The Adventures Of James Bond Junior 003½* by an unknown author under the pseudonym RD Mascott. The book featured Bond's namesake nephew.

Unbeknownst to the character, James Bond has a son, by Kissy Suzuki, in the novel *You Only Live Twice*.

Ian Fleming took the name "James Bond" from the author of a book, *Field Guides Of The Birds Of The West Indies*. The two men met in 1962.

The hero of Agatha Christie's *The Listerdale Mystery* is called "James Bond".

The first American paperback edition of *Casino Royale* was re-titled *You Asked For It*. Stunt co-ordinator Bob Simmons, not Sean Connery, is the first person to

appear on screen as Bond in *Dr No* in the opening gun-barrel sequence.

In 2006, Sean Connery had an asteroid named after him – 13070seanconnery.

The producers of the unofficial Bond movie *Never Say Never Again* considered approaching Roger Moore to play the part of M.

Christopher Lee, who played the villainous Scaramanga in *The Man With The Golden Gun*, is a cousin of Ian Fleming.

Sean Connery's younger brother Neil, a plasterer, appeared in the Italian-made 007 spoof *Operation Kid Brother*, along with *From Russia With Love* Bond girl Daniela Bianchi.

Rock singer Alice Cooper's 1974 album *Muscle of Love* contains a track, *The Man With The Golden Gun*, which Cooper claims was rejected as title song by the movie's producers.

Ian Fleming visited the set of *From Russia With Love* in Istanbul and legend has it he can be seen fleetingly in railway station sequences.

Heads of MI6 are known as "C", not M.

The character Goldfinger was named after the architect of the Trellick Tower, a 31-storey block of flats in Kensington.

The Man With The Golden Gun was the first Bond movie to be shown in the Kremlin.

Special-effects supervisor on *Thunderball* John Stears won an Academy Award for his work, but knew nothing about it until the Oscar arrived in the post.

Singer Tom Jones fainted in the studio after singing the final, high notes of *Thunderball*.

In the film *You Only Live Twice*, Mie Hama's character, Kissy Suzuki, is not named in the dialogue, only in the end credits.

Bond girl Jill St John, Tiffany Case in *Diamonds Are Forever*, has a genius-level IQ of 162 and was once wooed by American politician Henry Kissinger.

LEFT Breathless Bond singer Tom Jones

The *Daily Express* published prose adaptations of *Diamonds Are Forever* and *The Man With The Golden Gun* to tie in with the movie versions.

The scenes in which the first three Bonds throw their hats onto the coat rack often necessitated up to 12 retakes before the target was hit.

Publicist Tom Carlile convinced American censors not to re-name Pussy Galore "Kitty" when he arranged for a picture of Honor Blackman and Prince Phillip at the premiere of *Goldfinger* to be published in US newspapers under the caption "The Pussy and the Prince".

Gert Frobe's voice was dubbed as Goldfinger but he dubbed himself for the German version of the film.

Maud Adams can be glimpsed as an extra in the scenes at San Francisco's Fisherman's Wharf in *A View To A Kill*, making her third appearance in a Bond film.

Maryam d'Abo, Kara in *The Living Daylights*, screen-tested various candidates for replacement Bonds in 1981 when Roger Moore was considering retirement.

In Italy, *Dr No* was called *Licence To Kill*, so when the 1989 movie of that name was released its Italian title was *Private Revenge.*

The father of Pedro Armendariz, who plays General Lopez in *Licence To Kill,* played Kerim Bey in *From Russia With Love.*

Sean Bean, the villain Trevelyan in *GoldenEye,* was considered for the role of Bond after Timothy Dalton resigned.

The original title of *Tomorrow Never Dies* was "Tomorrow Never Lies" until a typographical error convinced the producers that the former sounded better.

At approximately 14 minutes, the pre-title sequence in *The World Is Not Enough* is the longest of any Bond movie.

Bond's Aston Martin DBS V12 rolled over seven times whilst the crash scene in *Casino Royale* was being filmed – a record.

Daniel Craig is the first James Bond to be younger than the series itself.

Other books also available:

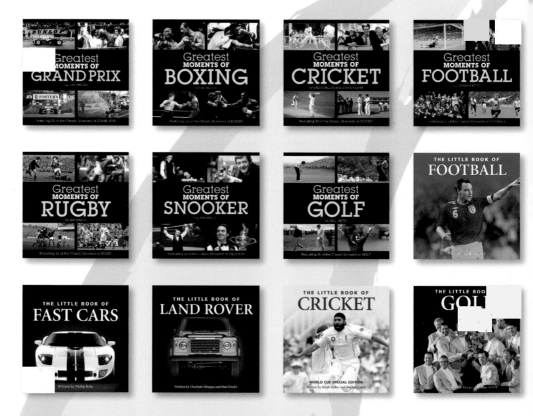

Available from all major stockists

GreenUmbrella Publishing

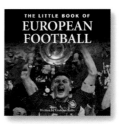

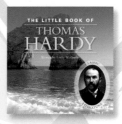

Available from all major stockists

The pictures in this book were provided courtesy of the following:

GETTY IMAGES
101 Bayham Street, London NW1 0AG

Design and artwork by David Wildish

Creative Director Kevin Gardner

Picture research Ellie Charleston

Published by Green Umbrella Publishing

Publishers Jules Gammond and Vanessa Gardner

Written by Michael Heatley & Mike Gent